ON THE WAY

On THE WAY

"...and how can we know the Way?"
"Jesus saith, I am the Way..."

BY ALVIN N. ROGNESS

Illustrated by
GEORGE RUNGE

Augsburg Publishing House
MINNEAPOLIS

ON THE WAY

Copyright 1942

AUGSBURG PUBLISHING HOUSE

MINNEAPOLIS, MINNESOTA

This volume is one in a series issued
by the Board of Parish Education

5240

Printed by the Augsburg Publishing House
Minneapolis, Minnesota

Manufactured in the United States of America

In Preface... MAN is a creature of eternity. God has given him an assignment in the world of time. This book is a discussion of the task that has been given him. It is neither a textbook of doctrine nor a guide to conduct, although it contains elements of each. It is rather a running discussion between the author and imagined groups of youth of those matters of Christian faith and life which derive from the Holy Scriptures and are summarized in Luther's Small Catechism. The prayer for the book would be answered if through its pages some young person would catch the epic of the Kingdom which by God's rich grace may be written in his swift years on this earth.

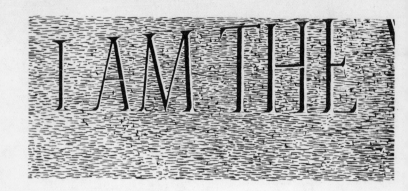

TABLE OF CONTENTS

Who am I?

CHAPTER 1 · "BELOVED, NOW ARE WE THE SONS OF GOD..."

You are the son of a King! But you are far from home!

Not many years ago your Father sent you out on this island called EARTH. *One day in the home palace He called you aside.*

HE said, "Son, out in the sea of space I have an island. I am about to send you out there for awhile. You will miss the home kingdom, I hope, and often long to be back. But I want you to visit this colony of Mine. Nor is it to be a vacation. I have work for you to do. I want you to transplant some of the justice and truth and love of the home kingdom to that island. Be not deceived, this task will not be an easy one. For many of your brothers and sisters already there have forgotten about Me and the task I have also given them. They will tell you it does not matter what you do. But remember that it does matter—a very great deal—to Me. You see, I love that island. Otherwise I should not have created it.

"It matters, too, because I have no one else to count on but you. I could have sent My angels out there to do this work.

1

"Looking unto Jesus, the author and finisher of our faith." Hebrews 12:2

But I send you, My sons and daughters, instead. If you do not work for justice, the earth will never know justice. If you do not love, no one there will know love. If you are not loyal to the truth, all will be error. I count on you. If you fail Me, war and poverty and crime will overrun the earth. All will be destruction and ruin.

"Nor must you forget that you are a King's son. You are a prince of the most royal house in the universe. I, your Father, am the King of kings and the Lord of lords. Each day be reminded of that. The instant you forget it, you are in danger. The enemy will overcome you. You carry the regal name, Christian. To let it be trampled in the dust will be your deepest shame; to carry its banner high will be your greatest glory.

"The particular job you will have is not My greatest concern. You may be a farmer or a shopman. You may become a teacher, a governor, or a pastor in My Church. Whatever honorable calling you follow, you will be working for Me. I am your real boss. Your trade or profession is but the field of labor, your corner of the vineyard. In that corner you will work for righteousness. Do not be over anxious about looking for faraway fields. Wherever you are, there you may work. There, right there, you may bring into your community the spirit and power of the home-kingdom.

2

"I will not leave you alone. I will be with you, even unto the end. My Church will be there, and the gates of hell shall not prevail against it. In My Church I will come to you through the Word and the Sacraments. Love and use them, and I will come to you and abide with you.

"Although you cannot see Me, you can speak with Me. I will hear. Pour out your sorrows and your joys; I will never be too busy to listen. No matter how trifling the need may be, ask of Me. Whatever is good for you, I will give. And whenever I do not give, have faith that I know best, and that all will work together for good if you but love Me.

"All will not be joy on this island. Long ago sin came and brought with it pain and sorrow and death. Many of the children whom I have sent out have rebelled against Me. You cannot altogether escape the contagion of that rebellion. Within your own soul you will have to struggle against it. The dread of doubt and failure will come over you. You will work with fear and trembling. But you need not be overcome by sin, for I Myself have overcome it for you. Centuries ago I gave My life on a cross to win victory and forgiveness for you.

"The greatest danger is that you may fall in love with this island so that you will not care to return to the home-kingdom. Love the island because it is My possession, but do not love it because it is your home. It is not your home! Your home is here in the palace with Me.

"Some day I will call you back. How soon, I shall not tell you. But one day I will usher you up to a doorway called death. Be not afraid of it, because on the other side of the threshold is Life. I will take you by the hand and lead you across. Then you shall see Me, face to face.

"Meanwhile, My peace I give you."

Who are we? Beloved, now are we the sons of God, and it doth not yet appear what we shall be!

THIS BOOK,

the Bible

*A person cannot believe in God without believing in the
Bible. For in the Bible God tells about Himself. It is God's
autobiography. More than that, God comes to man in the
Bible, just as surely as a friend comes to you in a car. Abraham
Lincoln once said, "I believe the Bible is the best gift God has
ever given to man. All the good from the Savior of the world
is communicated to us through this book." The world has always asked disturbing questions about this book. These questions can be answered satisfactorily only by one who is willing
to seek for God and have God seek for him. Let us ask some
of the most common of these questions.*

Can I believe anything for sure?

Yes, you can believe the Bible.

Why can I be sure the Bible is true?

Because it is God's book. God has inspired many fine writ-
ers, such as St. Augustine, Martin Luther, John Bunyan, and

4

"*. . . As they were moved by the Holy Ghost.*" II Peter 1:21

others. But the books they wrote were *their* books. We believe that in some unique manner the little books that Moses and Isaiah and Matthew and Paul and the rest wrote, sixty-six in all, were not their books, but together are *God's book*.

Do all men believe that the Bible is God's Word?

No. Many believe that the Bible is no more God's book than Aesop's Fables. These men believe that God never spoke to men, and that all we know about Him, His Will, and His Mercy, is what we and others have guessed or surmised about Him.

Can I prove that the Bible is God's Word?

You can be certain of it for yourself, but you cannot prove it to others. There is but one way of proving it: a person must himself prayerfully do what it commands and believe what it promises. Then, by God's grace, he will *discover* that it is God's Word. The Holy Spirit will open the door of certainty.

What else gives us assurance that it is the Word of God?

1. It claims for itself to be the Word of God (II Timothy 3:16).

5

2. Though it has sixty-six books, it has a remarkable unity of content, and is not self-contradictory.

3. Down through the centuries it has met the deepest needs of the individual, until now it is in part, at least, translated into over 1000 languages or dialects, and is consistently, year after year, the best seller.

What do some men trust instead of God's Word?

1. Some trust a man, such as a pope, a scholar, a sage, or a ruler. These people are sometimes called authoritarians.

2. Some trust their visions, experiences, or intuitions. They believe nothing except that which they have seen, felt or dreamed. They are sometimes called mystics.

3. Some trust their reason. They believe only that which they can understand or comprehend with their minds. They are sometimes called rationalists.

All may be helpful, and we should thank God for them. We should heed the thoughts and counsels of wise and good men. We should grow in experience and spiritual discernment. And we should exercise our reason as a gift from God. But none of these is the final authority. It is in God's Holy Word that we have the perfect revelation of Truth. And at the center of this revelation, the fullness of it, is Jesus Christ, the Word made flesh.

What if God had not revealed Himself in the Bible?

We would then be in the despair which one man describes, "Life is but a narrow vale between the cold and barren peaks of two eternities. We strive in vain to look beyond the heights. We cry aloud, and the only answer is the echo of our wailing cry." We believe in more than an echo; we believe in a Word from God. It is the Word that brings life, comfort, strength, and light. What we have in the Bible is not the wishful murmur of men; it is the Voice of God.

Was it not accident that brought sixty-six books together into the Bible?

To the unbeliever it looks like an accident. But the believer sees God's guiding hand in even that which seems accidental. The unbeliever is so troubled by what might have happened that he forgets what *did* happen. These books *did* survive the others; these books *did* receive the official sanction of the Church. And, for centuries, they now *have been* the source of knowledge, faith, and life.

How may I be helped to understand God's Word aright?

First, of course, by a willingness to obey its commands and believe its promises. But also by having a profound respect for what mature and learned Christians down through the centuries have believed the Scriptures to mean. That is the reason we hold Luther's Catechism in such high regard. We believe that the Catechism is a simple and thorough summary of the most important teachings of Scripture. But Dr. Luther, himself, more than any other person in history, insisted that every person who could read should be able himself to read the Word of God in his own language.

Is there any advantage in memorizing Scripture?

Great advantage. That which is once memorized and occasionally recalled becomes a fixed treasure in one's mind and heart. Many people, even if they have attended church regularly, perhaps never know more than the Lord's Prayer from memory. Their lives would be much enriched if they were sustained and comforted by memorized portions of God's Word. In the temptation in the wilderness, Jesus had the Word of God at His tongue-tip, and with that "two-edged sword" was able to drive off the evil one. It is not enough to have God's Word in our pockets or purses; we should have it in our memories, too.

The LAW and the GOSPEL

The Bible is divided into two parts, the Old and the New Testaments. Together they have sixty-six books. In each of these books there is Law; in each there is Gospel. If a man knows why God gave the Law and why He gave the Gospel, that man has Christian Knowledge. On the other hand, if a man knows the sixty-six books by heart, and DOES NOT know the difference between Law and Gospel, he does not have Christian Knowledge. In many ways, therefore, this is the most important chapter in our book.

Wherever the Bible tells man what he should do, there we have Law; wherever the Bible tells man what God has done for him, there we have Gospel. Both have for their final aim the salvation of man. Since the Fall, however, the Law cannot give man salvation; it can only prepare him for the Gospel. By showing man what he should do, but cannot do, the Law makes him ready to hear the glorious message of what God has already done for him in Christ.

8

All religions declare the Law; Christianity alone declares the Gospel

MAN was created with the Law written in his heart. This we call conscience. The Fall did not erase the Law completely from man's heart. Therefore, even the man-made religions have traces of God's Law in them, although the Bible alone reveals the perfect Law. Only the Christian religion has the Gospel, however. The story of God's love in Christ, His death and resurrection, and the forgiveness of sins for men—that we find alone in the Christian's Bible.

The Law commands; the Gospel offers

The Law says, "Thou shalt." In the Ten Commandments we have a statement of what God says we must do. Throughout the Scriptures He restates in many ways what He orders in the commandments. On the other hand, the Gospel tells us what God has done and is doing. It offers, full and free, the righteousness and forgiveness which Christ purchased and won for us. It tells how God came to earth in Christ, and how for thirty-three years He obeyed the Law perfectly. This perfect obedience He *gives* to us, through faith. The Gospel tells how God died on the cross and with His death purchased forgiveness of sins. He did not purchase it for Himself, for He had no sins to be forgiven. He purchased it for us. This forgiveness He *gives* us, again through faith. It is this amazing offer of God's gifts that constitutes the Gospel.

There is an IF in the Law; there is NO IF in the Gospel

The Law says, "*If* you do this, you shall be saved; *if* you will be perfect as your heavenly Father is perfect, you shall be saved; *if* you obey all the commandments all of the time, you shall be saved." The Gospel, on the other hand, promises free salvation. It asks nothing but this, "Take what I give, and you have it." The *if* of the Law is a terrible thing, because after the Fall no man can perfectly obey the Law. All have sinned and come short of the glory of God. The absence of the *if* in the

9

". . . Not of the letter, but of the spirit:

Gospel is its glory. There is no price to be paid, no conditions to be met; all men may have this salvation. God does not bargain away this salvation for something; He gives it away for nothing.

The Law threatens; the Gospel comforts

Wherever in Scripture you run across a threat, you may be sure that that passage belongs to the Law. Even old Christians sometimes forget this, and allow Satan to hurl the Law's threats at them. It is, however, true that only a man who has felt the terrors of the Law's threats can know the infinite comfort of the Gospel's promises.

The Law produces despair; the Gospel gives peace

The Law tells us what to do, but gives us no power to do it; it shows us our sins, but provides no triumph over them; it confronts us with the wrath of God and the terrors of hell, but suggests no way of escape. It leads, then, but to despair. The Gospel simply tells a story. It is the story of a God whc purchased pardon for sin for him, who won the victory over sin for him. And as it tells this story it goes further; it bestows the faith which believes it, accepts it, and lives by it. Despair is driven out of the heart; peace enters and dwells there.

The Law is for secure sinners; the Gospel is for alarmed sinners

As long as a person is not sorry for his sins, as long as he

For the letter killeth, but the spirit giveth life." II Cor. 3:6

remains at ease in them, as long as he is unwilling to quit some particular sin, so long the Law is for him. He needs to know the curse and the condemnation of the Law. However, the moment he becomes alarmed over his condition, then the Gospel is for him. He should then hear the glorious promises of God's rich grace.

✠

Some Scripture passages which are Law

"Thou shalt love the Lord, thy God, with all thy heart, and with all thy soul, and with all thy strength, and with all thy mind; and thy neighbor as thyself" (Luke 10:27).

"Cursed be he that confirmeth not all the words of this Law to do them" (Deut. 27:26).

"Be ye therefore perfect, even as your Father which is in heaven is perfect" (Matt. 5:48).

Some Scripture passages which are Gospel

"But he was wounded for our transgressions, he was bruised for our iniquities: the chastisement of our peace was upon him; and with his stripes we are healed" (Is. 53:5).

"For God so loved the world, that he gave his only begotten son, that whosoever believeth on him should not perish but have everlasting life" (John 3:16).

"This is a faithful saying and worthy of all acceptation, that Christ Jesus came into the world to save sinners, of whom I am chief" (I Tim. 1:15).

11

"I Believe..."

Not in ghosts, do you? Nor in goblins? Not even in Santa Claus!

It is fun to talk about them—in fables. But you do not believe in them, because you have never seen them. Nor has anyone else. They are only children of man's own imagination.

Some people say they will not believe in anything which they have not seen. Those people do not mean that, of course. They believe in Washington, and Jefferson, and Lincoln. They believe because someone else saw these men and wrote about them. They read about them, and learn to know them and believe in them.

Then, too, they believe in things no one has ever seen. They believe in love and hate even though no one has ever caught love and hate in a trap and looked at them.

Each Sunday you and millions of other people stand facing the altar and say, "I believe in God ...." But no man has

12

"*Lo, we have left all, and have followed Thee.*" Mark 10:28

seen God. For God is a Spirit, and your eyes cannot see the world of the spirit.

BUT once, long ago, God came down from His heaven and became man. His earthly name was Jesus. Men saw Him—Peter and James and John and many others saw Him. They beheld His glory, the glory as of the only begotten of the Father, full of grace and truth. Not all men beheld that glory, however. Many saw Him only as a carpenter, as a poor traveling preacher, or as an unfortunate fellow who was crucified one Friday near Jerusalem. They saw no more, because they used only their human eyes and did not have the eye of *faith*.

For thirty-three years God lived on earth. He lived without sin. He died innocent, for the sins of all men. Then He arose again, on Easter morning. Several weeks later He ascended to heaven in a cloud. He promised to come back some day, in a cloud. We are awaiting that day now.

Meanwhile, we confess that which we see through faith, "I

13

believe in God the Father, ... God the Son, ... God the Holy Ghost ...."

☩

It is a terrible thing to say, "I believe in God." When you say that you confess that you are willing to fear, and love, and trust in God above all things.

You fear God more than man. You have greater respect for Him than for the crowd; you stand in greater awe of Him than of the most powerful earthly ruler; you dread to displease Him more than you dread to displease your boss or your teacher or your folks.

You love God more than man. You love Him as a child loves his parents, only more. You love Him because He first loved you, and gave His life for you. Missionaries have gone to the uttermost parts of the earth, because they loved Him. Men have bestowed all their goods to feed the poor and have given their bodies to be burned, because they loved Him.

You trust God more than man. You count on Him more than you count on your father or mother. You have courage for the future not because of your friends, your money, or your ability, but because you know He stands by you. You have no self-confidence, but you have a towering God-confidence.

To believe in God means to entrust all into His care and keeping. It is as if you are an immigrant, standing on the pier ready to take passage. In your two bags is everything you own. Within you are your talents, your hopes, your loves, your ambitions. As you walk across the plank and stand on the deck of the ship, you entrust to the ship everything you are, everything you have, and everything you hope to be. To believe in God is to entrust all you have, all you are, and all you hope to be into the hands of One whom you have never seen. What a terrible risk! If He fails you, all is lost. But faith takes the risk, and makes the leap. You have committed all to Him.

For centuries millions of people have risked. They have not lost. They now have the crown incorruptible. You, catching their echo, join your little voice to the mighty chorus and say, "I believe in God ...."

14

WHAT

Is GOD *Like?*

---

*Most people picture God as a comfortable old Grandfather,
with a long grey beard, clothed in a flowing white night-gown.
Generally speaking, He is in good spirits. But sometimes He
becomes angry and sends earthquakes and war and rheuma-
tism to make people unhappy. He has angels to run His errands,
and His heaven is filled with old cranks who have never
learned to laugh.*

*Now, of course, that is not the Bible picture of God. In the
Scriptures God is pictured as Somebody so great and good
that words cannot describe Him. Nor can the small mind of
man even faintly grasp His glory. But there are pictures which
the Bible uses to give us some little glimpses into His being
and nature.*

He is like a Manufacturer

HE made all things, although He had *nothing* to make
them with. Because He did not have anything to start
with, His manufacturing is called creation. He simply
demanded that things come to be, and there they were! He

15

even made you and me, although we have earthly parents. Parents are but the method God used when He manufactured us.

He is like a King

He rules all things. He sets up laws. Natural laws govern that part of His creation which has no will. Spiritual or moral laws govern man, who has a will. In all His creation, there is but one lawbreaker—man. The wind, the sea, the birds, the beasts—all obey His law implicitly. Only man is disobedient.

He is like a Judge

Above all the courts of men there is a supreme court. Over it, God presides. The laws of this court are His laws. No man can escape standing before it. If he tries to run away, death will at last usher him before this bench.

He is like a Brother

When man stood before the Judgment and came under the sentence of eternal death for his sins, God was the Brother who took his place. Man was convicted and sentenced. Then God came, took man's sin upon Him, shouldered his guilt, and satisfied the demands of the eternal court by dying on Calvary. Man then stood no longer under the judgment of the Court; in the eyes of the Court man was innocent, without sin.

He is like a Shepherd

A shepherd loves his sheep, pursues them when lost, gathers them into the fold, and will die for them if need be. Because His sheep had strayed away, God came down to earth to seek them and save them. On the cross He laid down His life for them. Jesus Christ was God. The people who lived then did not know that He was God, nor have all people believed it since. But those who in faith have heard His voice have known.

He is like a Buyer

Man sold himself into the slavery of sin. The price which sin demanded was death. This price God paid on the cross when He redeemed man, when He bought him back from the dominion of sin. He bought him and set him free. Not all men have wanted to be free. Many have remained in slavery, even though they had been set free.

He is like a Father

He made us because He wanted us as His children. He has built us a home, and has opened the door. His greatest joy is to have His children live with Him; His greatest sorrow is to have them run away from Him. He provides for them like a father, He protects them like a father, He is merciful toward them like a father, and He punishes them like a father. No picture of God is employed in the Bible as often as that of the Father.

✠

NO picture of God is adequate. And were it not that God had walked the earth for 33 years as man, we would indeed be without much knowledge of Him. But in the four gospels we can follow Him through all sorts of situations. If we are willing to read and reread these accounts of His life, and in reading them allow the Holy Spirit to interpret them for us, we shall learn to know God.

When the world has asked, "What is God like?" the Christian Church has replied, "God is like Christ, for Christ was God." It was He who Himself said, "I and the Father are one . . . whosoever hath seen Me hath seen the Father." This is known as the great doctrine of the Incarnation. He is the Word, God, made flesh. The great God has not left Himself without a powerful witness on earth, for He was in Christ reconciling the world to Himself. And in the Scriptures, which chronicle His life on earth, man may stand face to face with the living, eternal God.

The GODS

Who Kill

There is one God.

But men make other gods. These man-made gods are monsters, and kill the people who worship them. Like ruthless dictators, when they sit on the thrones of men's hearts, they bring everything to confusion and destruction.

Man never seems to learn. Over and over again, in every age and place, he enthrones the wrong god. And over and over again, he gets into no end of trouble.

He knows that he should have no other gods before the one true God. He knows, too, that if he fears, loves, or trusts in any other god but the one true God, he is on the road to ruin. Still he persists in making gods of his own. Sometimes he hardly knows that he has other gods. He gives lip service to the true God, and deceives himself into thinking that he really worships the one God, but all the while he kneels at the altars of other gods. And as he kneels there, the false god, like a

18

demon, casts a spell over him and enslaves him. He is no longer free.

Pleasure

PLEASURE is a gift from the one true God. It was never intended to be a god itself, anymore than the sun or moon or wood or stone were intended to be gods. But when men make of pleasure a god, then all goes wrong. A boy who worships pleasure plays ball when he should be studying or working; he goes fishing or hunting when he should be in Sunday school or in church; he sees a movie when he should be helping his father or mother. He loves pleasure more than he loves the true God, you see, and without knowing it he has elevated pleasure to a throne in his heart. Sometimes a girl loves pleasure so much that she forgets her good name, she abandons her principles, she heeds neither God nor her parents. She *trusts* one pleasure after another for the happiness which only the true God can give. Finally she does anything and everything just to get a thrill. She has become a slave to the false god of pleasure.

Pleasure at last throws the soul aside into the pit of boredom. The thrills have become old, and the poor slave cannot get a "kick" out of anything anymore. Some years ago, Loeb and Leopold, two wealthy boys who had known all sorts of pleasures, killed one of their friends and pulled his body under a culvert to see if they might get a new thrill out of murder. Pleasure does not give happiness, nor does pain give unhappiness. God alone can make the human soul happy; to worship anything but the true God leads always at last to deep unhappiness, and to the soul's death.

Money

Money, too, is a trust from God. But it is not god. Men should not love it, trust it, or fear it. Many men do. They love it so much that they would do anything for it, lie, cheat, steal, and kill. They trust it too. They count on it to get them out of trouble, to keep them in health, to provide them with power, to win them friends, to assure them a good name. They even fear it. They stand in dread of losing their own money. They stand in awe of other men who have much money.

This god is dreadfully deceitful. For though he seems to promise all kinds of freedom to those who will worship him, yet his people always end up by being galley slaves. How many rich men there are who do not give to the poor and support the church, simply because they no longer can decide for themselves to do it! When someone asks them for a gift, they cannot say "yes"; their god will not let them. This god will let them spend money for evil things, or even lavish it foolishly upon themselves and their family. Sometimes he will not even let them do that. Like the Houglums in Rolvaag's *Pure Gold,* they may even be compelled to starve and freeze because their god tells them they must.

Every man is daily invited to worship at his shrine. And millions do. Little boys will not run errands for their mothers without pay. Young men choose their vocations in life simply because this job or that one will pay them well. Grown men forget about their families, neglect to go to church or read the Bible, tax their bodies and minds overtime, simply to pick up some extra money. Girls will date a man for his money, will marry him for his money, and will continue through life to prod him on to make more and more money.

This god perhaps has more followers than any other. Men who have wealth worship him because they want to keep the wealth they have; men who are poor worship him because they want to get the wealth they yet do not have. Jesus once said that the love of this god was the root of all evil. He pointed out, further, that to break the grip of this god was so hard that it was easier for a camel to go through the needle's eye than for a rich man to enter the Kingdom of Heaven.

Popularity

It takes a strong man not to worship this god. By nature everyone wants to be liked, wants to be honored, wants other people's praise. Whenever a person wants these things so much that he will disobey or forget God to get them, he has become a worshipper of popularity. One football player wants a better write-up than another; a girl tries to look prettier than her friends; a housewife works hard to bake a better cake than her neighbor; a doctor wants to hear that he is a better physician than his rival; a minister is tempted to listen for the praise of his people. Sometimes we call all this striving ambition, or competition, and we think that it is all right. But whenever a man does a thing well in order to get ahead of some other man, he probably has the wrong god. A man should do things well, not because he wants to outdo his friends or enemies, but simply because it is the will of the one true God that he do things well. If he worships the true God, he will seek to please and honor Him above all things. A boy should play ball well, study hard, work diligently, spend and save wisely not to get ahead of his fellows, but because God wants him to do all things well. A girl should be pleasant and helpful, look clean and neat, acquire the graces of good breeding, not in order to climb higher than her friends on the social ladder, but because her God wishes her to exercise care in all things. Such a person lives honorably among men, to be approved of God. He may like popularity, but he worships God.

✝

A CHRISTIAN may enjoy the many pleasures of life to their full, he may grow wealthy, and he may win the praise and popularity of men. But these remain for him the incidentals of life. At life's center, deep within his heart, his decisions are governed by the will of God. He fears, loves, and trusts the one true God above all things.

The Windows of

WORDS

You cannot always judge a man by his language. Even a bad man may sometimes use pious words. In the Garden of Gethsemane, Judas addressed Jesus by the respectful title, "Master," the very moment he betrayed Him. Some time before, the Lord had warned Judas and the others that anyone could talk reverently, but that "not everyone that saith Lord, Lord, shall enter the Kingdom of Heaven." Most important, He continued, a man must DO *the will of the Father.*

There are people who on Sunday morning in church confess their sins, sing the glorias, and declare their faith, and all the while they have no genuine reverence for God in their hearts. Still worse, there are people who whisper His name as they face the altar in worship on Sunday, and bark out His name when they become angry on Monday.

To a Christian, both speech and behavior will express the inner life God has given him. It is really just as irregular to expect a Christian to use his tongue in blasphemy as to expect him to use his hands in murder.

22

Words are windows

ONLY God knows what is in a man's heart. Sometimes, however, what a man says and does gives us a little glimpse into his soul. Especially is this true of what he says and does when he is off guard. A man usually does not deliberately plan to swear or curse. Usually he does it without thinking. Precisely for this reason is it that blaspheming God's name is so serious. For it opens a window to what the man in his heart thinks of God. No one uses lightly or disrespectfully the name of a person he loves or fears. A lover speaks the name of his beloved only in highest devotion and respect. A son honors and esteems the name of his mother. Similarly, if a man really loves, fears, and trusts in God, it is inconceivable that he will toss God's name around carelessly on the football field, or in the shop, or on the streets. In early Israel, the worshipper would not even speak God's name in the temple, because he did not feel worthy to utter the name of Him who was so great and exalted.

Behind the words

Behind the words are meanings. And meanings tell the story of how a man thinks—what he is. Let us examine some of the everyday expressions of blasphemy, and, if we can, find the story behind them.

"God damn you"; "Damn it." This is a wish, or a prayer. A man asks God something. To be proper, he really ought to fold his hands when he says it. He prays God to send someone to hell. It is a terrible thought that many men pray to God every day, and that the only request they ever send to the throne on high is a prayer that someone may be sent to hell. It is hard to believe that such a person has any real belief either in heaven or hell, God or Satan, salvation or judgment.

"Aw hell." No one loves hell or the devil, of course, but every Christian knows that they are dreadfully real. They are his enemies, and he should know better than to speak of or treat them lightly. There is nothing the devil likes better than

23

to have people play around with him, make jokes about him, and let his name trip lightly over their tongues. For he knows that he can much more easily overcome a person who does not take him seriously. It is therefore that a person who speaks frivolously of the devil and hell gives Satan pleasure and God pain.

"By God." A person may testify by calling God to witness only when the court or some solemn occasion demands it. To emphasize the truth of a thing by thoughtlessly saying, "By God, it's so," is to make the oath a thing of no consequence, and thus to bring God's holy name into disgrace.

"Jesus Christ." God gave to Jesus "a name which is above every name, that at the name of Jesus every knee should bow, of things in heaven, and things in earth, and things under the earth, and that every tongue should confess that Jesus Christ is Lord, to the glory of God the Father" (Philippians 2:9). In the United States no national character is as esteemed as Abraham Lincoln; and no good citizen would dare to throw his name around carelessly or disdainfully. But every day the name of Christ is uttered in jest or in anger by thousands of thoughtless people. The name of the worst criminal or the most tyrannical ruler has never been trampled in the dust as is daily the name of the King of kings and the Lord of lords.

The petty offenders, "Gee" or "Gee whiz," are probably genteel adaptations of the name Jesus. "Gosh" and "Golly" are substitutes for "God." "Darn" is a weakened form of the word "damn." "For goodness' sake" implies "For Christ's sake," since He is the author of all goodness. It scarcely matters what "by-word" one uses, usually such words relate themselves to God and eternity. The fact that man insists on using words of this kind is evidence of the deep rebellion in man's heart. And every man, young and old, must constantly be on guard so that he does not heap scorn and ridicule upon the name of the great God, the name above all others he ought rather to honor and revere.

The LORD'S Day

God has seven days in each week. All seven are His. Monday is as much His day as Sunday, Tuesday as Wednesday. But to help man order his life well, God early singled out one day to be used differently from the rest. On this day man was to rest from his work, and use his leisure for the refreshing both of body and soul.

Jesus laid down no hard and fast rules for Sabbath behavior. From His life, however, we know He used the Lord's Day for rest, for worship, and for loving service.

This matter of rest

SOME people must work on Sunday. The pastor must preach on Sunday, the farmer must feed his cattle on Sunday, the cook in a restaurant must prepare food on Sunday, the nurse must care for the sick on Sunday. But there is much work that need not be done on Sunday at all. Most factories could close for one day, most stores could stop their

"Let us meet together in the house of God,

business, and most men could even do their odd jobs on some other day. Many firms and people, however, slip into the habit of working on Sunday, and after awhile believe that they must. Nor do the rest of the people help them change their habits. Most gasoline stations, for instance, could be closed on Sundays if we would remember to buy our gasoline on Saturdays, as we do our groceries.

People who make use of Sunday for rest are usually the happiest people. There are students who plan so that they never have to study on Sunday, and become better students because of it. There are men who close their stores and shops on Sunday, even at a loss of money, and are the happier in their work. There are boys who give up Sunday caddying or a Sunday newspaper route, so that they can take a full part in the church's program. All these people receive special blessing, because at a sacrifice they set the day aside for God.

This matter of attending church

There are kind and respectable people who rarely, if ever, attend church. They seem to get along in life just as well as those who do go to church. They may be just as intelligent,

within the temple." Neh. 6:10

just as cheerful, just as generous. But they are missing one of God's greatest gifts. For it is in church, through His Word and His Sacraments, that God comes to people with His law and gospel. And it is in church that the people come together regularly to adore and praise and thank God. Men may read His Word by themselves, of course; and they may praise and thank Him by themselves. But it is reasonably sure that a man who neglects to hear God's Word in church on Sunday will also neglect to read His Word at home; and the man who cannot set aside an hour to thank God in the communion of his fellow-believers, will not set aside much time for thanksgiving during the week either. The church worship is another of God's fine gifts whereby He helps us remember Him.

There are good reasons for going to church, and poor ones. A person should not attend church merely because his friends go, or because he likes the preacher or his preaching, or because he can hear fine music. He goes, first, to hear God's Word. This he hears both in the liturgy and in the preaching. As long as the preacher declares God's Word and not false teaching, it does not matter to the worshipper whether he personally likes the preacher or his style of preaching. He did not come to church to hear the word of the minister, you see; he

27

came to hear the Word of God. Secondly, he goes to thank and praise God. This he can do whether the music is good or not, whether the sermon is especially interesting or not, whether he meets his friends there or not. He has set the hour aside for God, not for himself. He comes to worship.

Nor does the Christian worshipper allow anything to prevent his meeting this weekly appointment with his God. Only sickness or emergency circumstances can keep him from church. If sudden company arrives, he invites them to come with him; if he is on a trip, he seeks some church worship on the way; if he must work in the morning, he attends in the evening. He does not treat lightly this high privilege God has given him. For him, it is neither too cold in the winter nor too warm in the summer. Like his pioneer grandfather, he lets neither storm from without nor laziness from within keep him from church.

Although the pastor may have assigned no lesson for the Sunday worship, the Christian will prepare for it, nevertheless. He should read the texts for the day before he reaches the worship, preferably during the first part of the week. He should pray for his pastor, that the Holy Spirit may be permitted to lead him in the preparation of the sermon. He should pray for himself, that his soul might be the good soil, in which the Word finding root may bear a hundredfold. He should even guard himself during the week, especially Saturday evening, so that he does not come to the worship with a weary body and a sluggish mind.

In the congregation, nothing is as central as the Sunday worship. A person who is diligent in Luther League, in Sunday school, or in any of the organizations of the church, but who is negligent at worship, is a poor church member. But what is more tragic, such a person loses the blessings of the occasion where old and young, men and women, rich and poor, gather in the presence of God as the fellowship of believers, guided in worship by their pastor, the shepherd of the flock.

28

GOD'S
Vice-Presidents

God has His finger on everything. A sparrow cannot fall to the ground without His knowledge. Since He is all-knowing, all-wise, all-powerful, all-good, and everywhere-present, it might seem that He would govern everything without any helpers. But He has vice-presidents. These He asks us to respect and obey. Only when they command us to do that which is specifically contrary to God's will are we privileged to disobey them.

Father and Mother

THESE are God's first vice-presidents. They normally should, and most often do, love you more than any other. God has given them first charge over us. It is their duty first to want us, even before we are born. Some husbands and wives do not want children. In this they sin grievously against the Creator. Most of our parents, however, have begun loving us before birth. Most of them continue loving us till death, however many times we fail them. Parents are to see that we

29

"Thou madest him to have dominion over the works of thy hands;

are fed, clothed, and sheltered. But we are both body and soul. Therefore, they must above all see that the soul is fed with the bread of life, that the soul is clothed in the full armor of God, and that it is sheltered under the wings of the Almighty.

Because they have such a high office, God is especially concerned that we love, respect, and obey them. Scripture is full of praise for the obedient child and of blame for the disobedient. Nor should we forget to thank them. Forgetfulness is the cruelest of all weapons. To forget to say kind things to them, to forget to write them, to forget to come to them when they grow old,—these break a mother's and father's heart.

God asks us to honor them. To honor a Christian parent one must himself live a Christian life. The finest tribute a good parent can receive is the life of a good child. No monument or gift can take the place of that.

The Pastor

Next to the home, no earthly place is as exalted as the Christian congregation. Over the congregation, the Lord has

thou hast put all things under his feet." Psalm 8:6

placed a shepherd, the pastor. His salary is paid by the people, but he is called by, works for, and takes orders from, God. He is an ordinary human being like the rest, but the Lord of the Church has placed him at the head of the assembly of believers. He prays for his people; his people should pray for him.

The Teacher

There are teachers in public schools, and there are teachers in the church school. Each is charged with teaching the Truth. Few, if any, callings are as high as that of the teacher. Many public school teachers work for small salaries; most Sunday school teachers work for no salary at all. We respect and honor them by studying carefully the assignments they give, by giving attentive heed to what they teach, by following whatever good counsel they give and by showing them kindness and gratitude.

Government Officials

Governments are of God, and rulers are servants of God. They administer the law. The source of all law is the Ten

Commandments. A man who obeys the law of the land need not fear the president, the king, the governor, the judge, or the police. The Christian obeys the law even when no one is looking, because he knows God is looking and is pleased to have him obey. Sometimes there are evil rulers, who command people to do evil things. Then we are to obey God rather than man, because God is our great ruler. Daniel disobeyed Darius; Moses disobeyed the Pharaoh; the wise men disobeyed Herod. History is full of the stories of martyrs who went to their death rather than obey wicked rulers in that which was wrong.

Employers

Most men work for someone. They have a boss, an employer, a manager, or a superintendent, who gives orders. If they do not obey, they may lose their jobs. The Christian obeys not primarily because he is afraid of losing his job, however, but because God wants him to be a good worker, a respectful employee. To work hard, to take a personal interest in the welfare of the business, to be sympathetic with the employer's problems are all characteristics of a Christian employee.

Over All

We must obey God rather than man. Sometimes parents set their children poor or bad examples; sometimes pastors are false shepherds and lead their flocks into error and not into truth; there are teachers who teach lies; there are rulers who use their power for injustice; there are employers who have no honest regard either for life or property. In every situation the Christian is governed by God. Sometimes he obeys man because he loves God; sometimes he disobeys man because he loves God. In all things he conforms himself first and always to the will of God. For God is his Father; God is his Shepherd; God is his Teacher; God is his Ruler; God is his Master. If the vice-president's order is contrary to the President's, the Christian obeys the President.

The Sacredness
of LIFE

CHAPTER 10 · "THOU SHALT NOT KILL"

Life seems short, even to the man who lives eighty years. The years slip by swiftly, and soon it is over.

Each day is important—and each year. However long or short one's life might be, all of it has importance. For the life we live on earth is our "working day" for the Lord in His enterprises on earth.

No man has a right to shorten that "working day," either for himself or for others. Only the Lord Who gave life has a right to determine when that life should end.

No man lives on indefinitely

SINCE sin came, no man can live here forever. No matter how careful he is of his health, someday he will die. Nor would any person really desire to live on earth forever. There is too much pain, sorrow, and distress for anyone to wish that. People have sought "the fountain of perpetual youth" in vain. Had there been such a stream or spring, and had someone found it, he would have been bored with the years as they came and went. Since the Fall, there is a deep

"Be not afraid . . . of the desolation of the wicked." Prov. 3:25

groaning and travailing in all men—a strange longing for deliverance from a life so beset with sin. No man would honestly want it to keep on forever.

Life itself not the highest good

Any Christian should know that there are some things worth more than life. Down through the years men have walked to certain death rather than surrender those things. It is a tragedy when men think that the most important thing in life is simply to live. However, life itself is one of God's gifts, and as a gift from Him should be held in earnest trust. No one should deliberately waste life, neither his own nor another's.

A temple for the soul

The body is the dwelling place for the soul; and if the soul belongs to God, it is the dwelling place for the Spirit of God. As such it has peculiar value. Nothing should defame it, nor weaken it, nor destroy it. The life of the body becomes precious therefore because it has become, or can become, the earthly abode of the eternal God.

Destroying the temple

A house can go to ruin either by what you do or by what you do not do. You can put some dynamite in the basement

"None of them that trust in him shall be desolate." Psalm 34:22

and blow it to bits, or by neglecting to repair it or care for it you can let it gradually fall apart.

A man's body can be destroyed by drink or lust or gluttony; it can be destroyed by simply disregarding the ordinary rules of health and sanitation. In either event, you kill the body.

A man may kill someone by shooting a bullet into his heart; he may kill someone by driving carelessly on the highway; he may kill someone by refusing to share food with him when he is hungry.

Our country, even in peace time, has a terrible crime record. It is estimated that crime costs our nation $150,000,000 more each year than the total amount spent for education and church and charity. And our deaths from automobile accidents alone have in a single year been over 30,000, more than the total number of our boys killed in the first World War. As a nation, we have a shameful record in the stewardship of life.

Caring for one's own temple

Every careless habit of health is a neglect of God's gift of life. Every needless risk is a wanton waste of opportunity for service on God's earth. There are conditions, however, which require risks. A doctor who shortens his own life because of faithful service to the sick does not commit suicide. Nor does a pastor who gives unstintingly of himself in the work of the

35

Kingdom. Nor does any person who is untiring in his labors of love for others. And surely a missionary who risks his life among enemies and is killed in so doing, cannot be said to be wasting his temple.

Caring for another's temple

Jesus said that His people would be busy giving food to the hungry, drink to the thirsty, clothes to the naked, and care to the sick. He Himself had endless compassion for the physical needs of the people about Him. He made sure that His people would realize that the soul was far more important than the body; but He made equally sure that His people would not forget to be alert to the simple bodily needs of their fellow men. A Christian father is concerned about the bodily needs of his family; a Christian employer is faithful in caring for the everyday needs of his employees; a Christian citizen is alert to prevent poverty and sickness among all people of his community. Toward friend and foe alike, the follower of Christ shows a deep concern for needs of the body. Crime and poverty and war and pestilence and famine—all these enemies of life—become his enemies. For they constantly threaten the earthly temple of God's eternal spirit.

The inner enemy

Jesus said that hatred was the real enemy of life. The man who hates has really already committed murder in his heart, said Jesus. As love is the giver and keeper of life, so hate is the thief and destroyer of life. The person who holds a grudge or plans revenge or refuses to forgive has in his heart the spirit of the killer. Jesus told His followers that it was their duty not only to rid their own hearts of hatred but also to do everything in their power to drive hatred out of their enemies' hearts too. If someone holds a grudge against you, even if you are not at all to blame, it is your Christian duty to go to him and by patience and kindliness to break down ill-will. It was thus that the Lord Himself did. While we were yet enemies of His, not because of anything He had done against us (for we were the rebels, in selfishness against His will), He came and gave His life on the cross to win us back to Him.

God can take life

God gave life, and God can take it back. In the deepest sense, God never intended man to die. Death came, not because of, but in spite of, God. It was the Lord's original intention that man should live in unbroken fellowship with Him, without sorrow, sickness, or death. When sin came, death came. Since then, God has used death as the gateway to the full eternal fellowship He had planned for man from the beginning. Some day He will usher us through the passageway of death into that greater Life. Our earthly temple will be laid away to rest until the Resurrection Day, when it will be restored again as the soul's dwelling. At death the soul moves out of the temple; at the Resurrection it moves back in.

One day John Quincy Adams, then over 70, was walking in the garden. A friend asked him, "How's John Adams today?" He replied, "John Adams himself is very well, thank you, very well. The dwelling he has inhabited these 70 years, however, is beginning to show the strain of the years. It is crumbling here and there, sagging at the corners, and sways and creaks in the storms. Soon John Adams will be summoned to leave these quarters. But John Adams himself is very well, thank you . . . very well!"

When a
Man's a M<small>AN</small>

CHAPTER 11 · "THOU SHALT NOT COMMIT ADULTERY"

A real man is a fighter. He fights for the right. He dares to stand alone, against the whole crowd. He is not a coward, even when people laugh at him.

A real man is a worker. He does not shirk his studies or his job. On the football field, or on the basketball court, he gives the best that is in him. No one can call him a chiseler or a piker.

But you can tell whether he is really a man or not best by how he treats girls and women. That is the final and supreme test.

A real man protects women

MEN are stronger than women. A man may therefore attack and overcome women; or he may protect and shield them. Any man naturally protects his mother or his sister or his daughter. But it takes a real man to protect everybody's mother and sister and daughter. A man should

38

treat all girls as he would like to have other men treat his sister or his mother.

Within himself, a real man is not a galley slave; he is a general

Every healthy man has strong desires. Sometimes these desires try to order him around. They tell him to do something low. But a real man does not take orders from these passions. He commands them; he is their general. They cannot drive him around like a common galley slave. He is not the errand boy for his desires. He is their master, and puts them in their place. Sometimes when he is with girls these passions try to get the best of him. But a real man will watch and pray, he will be on guard, and won't let them boss him around.

A real man is shrewd

He knows you cannot harvest wheat if you plant thistle. He knows you cannot live a clean life if you plant unclean thoughts. Therefore he is on guard with his mind. He does not hunt around for pictures of naked women in the magazines. He does not attend the movies that excite his desires. He does not laugh at smutty stories, nor does he tell them. If his friends want to go into dives or taverns, he tells them he'll see them later. But he is not a goody-goody. He simply is shrewd, and knows that no one can play around with low thoughts very long and keep his life on a high level. For that reason he reads good books, travels with a decent crowd, and keeps busy with wholesome activities. Nor does he forget to go to church and Sunday school, to read his Bible, and to pray. For he knows that he needs the constant help of God if he is not to slip.

Even a father will trust a real man

The finest tribute that any man will give you is that he trusts you to take care of his daughter. A real man, therefore, is not afraid of his girl friend's dad. Because, you see, such a young man really is helping to guard and protect his daughter.

A real man looks forward to a family of his own

Even a boy of thirteen or fourteen, just awakening to his sex powers, begins to dream of some girl whom he will love enough to marry. Together, if God gives them health, they will have children of their own. He wants his wife and these children to be proud of the kind of man he is, and the kind of man he has been. So he lives clean for the sake of those who some day will be his. He does not squander these fine sex powers; he controls and commands them. They are set aside for his own future home and family.

A real man is clean because God counts on him

Long ago in Egypt, Joseph was tempted to commit adultery with Potiphar's wife. He lost his job and was thrown into prison because he refused. He refused, because he knew God counted on him to do the right. He said, "How can I do this great wickedness, and sin against God?" Like Joseph, a real man is clean not because he is afraid, but because he knows God is counting on him to go clean. That is the reason, above all other reasons, why he must keep himself physically strong, mentally awake, and morally straight.

> "To every man there openeth
> A way, and ways, and a way;
> The high soul climbs the high way,
> The low soul gropes the low,
> And, in between, on the misty flats,
> The rest drift, to and fro.
> But to every man there openeth
> A high way and a low.
> And each man must choose
> The way his soul shall go."
>
> —OXENHAM.

40

The KIND *of Girl*

Men Marry

Two college students were sitting in the library whispering. They were discussing girls, and comparing notes. They dismissed one after another with such remarks: "Aw, she's not so good, anybody can kiss her"; "She's o. k. if you want a hot date, but she's dumb"; "She can dance and pet, but that's about all you can say for her"; "Anybody can paw all over her." Finally they came to one, Mary. One of the boys said, "There's a girl for you; I've had at least a dozen dates with her, and I haven't even put my arm around her. She's too swell to be cheap." And the other replied, "Boy, that's the kind of a girl I'm going to marry."

Men do not marry public property

SOME men are strange creatures. They seem willing to date any kind of girl if she is good looking, but when they look for someone to marry they become terribly "choosy." They want someone with high ideals and good character. They will pass by the flashy girl who has been in the arms of every Tom, Dick, and Harry, and will select some

41

"Strength and honor are her clothing,

girl with less dash, whose caresses have not been lavished upon all comers. These men, many of them, probably do not deserve the love of a fine girl, but they will look for her and woo her, nevertheless. You see, when a man marries he wants a girl who can be the queen of his home, the mother of his children, an encouragement and inspiration to him.

The girl who is "tops" does not buy or sell dates

Many a young man will take a girl to a show if he can fondle her a while afterward. But no first-rank girl will sell her kisses for a date. She will rather go without dates and be called unpopular than make such a bargain. There are low women who will sell themselves, their honor and all, for a few dollars. They are called harlots, and are the castaways of society.

A good girl knows the difference between popularity and esteem

There are popular girls whom no first-rate man wants to marry. And there are unpopular girls whom all men esteem

42

and she shall rejoice in time to come." Prov. 31:25

and honor and wish they could marry. For, you see, a girl can become popular by being cheap; but she cannot receive honor and esteem by being cheap.

Any girl has great power

Though physically much stronger, men are nevertheless governed by their women. A man often will be as good as his mother, his sister, or his sweetheart wants him to be. If they are careless with their power, they can set him on the road to ruin. If they possess high Christian ideals, they, more than any earthly power, can lead him in the path of those ideals. Many a boy has become a great and good man because he has had a noble mother, a lovely sister, or a good, wholesome sweetheart. A woman is a leader of men.

A good girl plans for her own home

At about twelve years a girl begins to change into a woman. Dreams then begin to fill her mind. She dreams of the time when some fine, manly man will love her, and will want her to be his bride. But she does more than dream; she *plans,* too. She lays plans to be ready for that time. Each day she keeps herself morally clean for him who will some day come for her. She wants to be able to give him a clean and pure love, so that she can be worthy of the clean and pure love he will offer her.

A good girl remembers God's high place for her

God wants her to be pure. Even if all the world should want her to forget her ideals, and only God should still want her to be pure, a Christian girl would stand firm. For after all, what God wants is the most important consideration for the Christian. It may be that no man would come to claim her, and she would have no home of her own. That would not change her course, because it was above all for God that she lived a pure life. As a Christian she belongs to the Lord's bride, His Holy Church, and shall some day be claimed by Him.

"Above the Snake Line"

Long ago some colonists were settling in New England. They found a beautiful valley and were about to build their homes there, when suddenly they discovered that the ground was infested with poisonous snakes. They dared not live there, that they knew! As they plodded upward toward the plateau, they noted that the snakes were fewer and fewer, until finally they reached a level where the snakes were gone altogether. There they built their homes, cleared the ground, and planted their crops. They settled *above* the snake line.

There is a snake line in life, too. No wise girl will dwell below it. For there she finds indecent companions, cocktails, questionable amusements, and many other "snakes" which endanger the life of her soul. True, it may be possible to dwell there and not be bitten, but it is not probable. The risks are too great. Her life with God is at stake, her good name is at stake, her future happiness and well-being are at stake. So she prays, "Lead us not into temptation," and in thought and habit builds her life above the snake line.

A Common

THIEF

CHAPTER 13 · "THOU SHALT NOT STEAL"

Johnny had not intended to steal that day. But before night he had stolen four times.

Here is how it happened:

In the bathroom he found a dime. It had rolled out of his dad's pocket when he took a bath. Johnny thought, "How lucky," and thrust it in his pocket. His dad would never miss it, and how Johnny could use it! That was theft number one: he had stolen ten cents from his dad.

On the school playground, and only two minutes before the bell! He would not get his turn at bat, so he "horned in" ahead of Jim, and swung at the ball just as the bell rang. Theft number two: he had stolen a turn from his pal.

Miss Jones had carefully explained the problem in algebra. But Johnny had been day-dreaming. When she asked him to do the problem, he said, "I did not understand it." She explained it again, and he listened, and learned it. But he had stolen four minutes of the teacher's time. Theft number three!

"Whatsoever things are true . . . honest . . . think on these things."
Phil. 4:8

In the afternoon he sat writing an English quiz. He could not remember the answer to the third question. He sat for five minutes, trying to think. But he just could not remember! So he glanced over at Jane's paper, and there it was. He could not help seeing it. He scribbled the answer, and handed in his paper. Theft number four: he had stolen knowledge from Jane.

Let us ask some questions about thieves and thefts.

Who is the real owner of all things?

God. Even the Morgans, Rockefellers, and Duponts have no real property. They, and we, manage God's property. We may be good managers, or bad. We may guard all things for God, or we may steal all things from God.

If we are not owners, what are we?

Stewards, managers, or trust-officers. Most people forget that. Long ago Jesus told of a farmer who forgot. He had built new granaries and cribs, and they were running over. He was rich. He forgot who really owned the grain, and sat back to enjoy it all. Then God suddenly called him up for the accounting, and fired him. He told him, "Thou fool, this night thy soul is required of thee." The next day he would no longer be in charge. He would be gone, and he could take nothing with him.

Guardians of Property

Every day we use property that belongs to someone else. The sidewalks we walk on are not ours; the school chairs we sit in are not ours; the library books we read are not ours. Over all these things we are custodians. We should not throw waste paper on the walks, or carve our names on our desks, or tear the pages of books we read. As good citizens of the Kingdom and of our community, we should treat with care all property that we use.

Can a man steal from God?

Of course he can, just as easily as a banker may embezzle the funds of a depositor. If your father deposits $5,000 in a bank, he does not *give* that money to the banker. He asks the banker to invest the money for him, to put it to work for him. Suppose a year later your father should come for the money, and the banker should say, "The money is no longer here; I used it for my family." What would your father think? Your father would say, "I've been robbed!"

God has deposited something with you. He has left with you a body and a mind, time and energy. It is not your body; it is God's. It is not your mind, nor your time, nor your energy. It is God's. He expects you to invest it all for Him. And one day He will ask to see your accounts, so that He may check over how you managed His things.

47

Does God care how I spend my money?

You should get money honestly; and you should spend money honestly. A man who squanders money on himself is a thief before God, just as surely as a man who breaks into someone's locker to steal from another. A boy in high school usually does not earn much money. But he spends money. Suppose he spends $1.00 one week:

For baseball bat	50 cents
For ice cream	10 cents
For a show	15 cents
For gum	5 cents
For malted milk	10 cents
For candy	5 cents
For church offering	5 cents

Is there anything wrong with the account? Do you think God would say that he had invested this dollar wisely for God that week? Every young boy or girl who spends money at all ought to manage his spending for God. And in that spending surely the church offering should have a regular and prominent place, if God is to find us faithful stewards and managers.

One-tenth to the Lord

In the Old Testament Church the people observed the "tithe." They gave ten per cent of all they earned to the Lord. Many Christians today give on that basis too; and it is probably safe to say that those who tithe are the happiest givers of all.

Who is the greatest thief?

The man who forgets God altogether. If he uses his time as if it were his own, if he employs his abilities as if they belong to him, if he spends his money as if it were his alone, he steals his whole life from God.

The TRAIL

of a LIE

Benjamin Franklin once said, "Honesty is the best policy." In more modern language, we say "honesty pays." But the Christian tells the truth whether it pays or not, simply because God wants him to tell the truth. Usually one can tell the difference between a Christian and a non-Christian by this rule: a non-Christian will do good if it pays him to do good; a Christian will do good not because it pays, but because his Lord asks him to do good.

The father of lies

IT was a lie that started man's trouble on earth. Satan, the father of lies, disguised as a serpent, lied to Eve. He told her that God did not mean what He had said about the tree of knowledge, and that if she ate of the fruit she would not die. That, of course, was not true. To their great sorrow, Eve and Adam discovered that it was a lie. God is the author of truth and Satan is the father of lies; and man may choose the kind of family and the sort of life he wishes to share, God's or Satan's.

49

"... *Every idle word that men shall speak,*

Lie upon lie

An untruth does not generally come alone. If you entertain one, you usually have to make room for all his friends. One night John had gotten his father's car to attend the Luther League. Instead, he went to a neighboring town to a party. Upon returning home, his father asked, "Did you attend the League meeting?" and John said "Yes." (Lie number one.) His father continued, "Did you see Bob there?" to which John replied, "Yes." (Lie number two.) His mother asked, "Did you enjoy the program?" and John said, "Yes, I thought it was good." (Lie number three.) "But it took you a long time to come home," his father said, and John explained, "The gang played games quite late, and I had some trouble getting the car started." (Lies, four and five.)

You see, once a person takes to the path of lying, it is hard to do other than go on, further and further.

This thing called gossip

We must be extremely careful not to say anything about a person unless we know for sure that it is true. The good name, or reputation, of a person may be damaged by people reporting something as true which they do not know to be true. One day Mary thought she saw Jane cheating in an examina-

50

they shall give account thereof in the day of judgment." Matt. 12:36

tion. She told it to her friends. Soon the whole town was talking about it. The teacher heard about it, and called Jane aside to ask her. But Jane had not cheated. So the teacher began tracing down the lie, and at last discovered that Mary had started the story. Mary was very sorry, and was anxious to undo her wrong. The teacher took her out on the lawn, picked up a dandelion plant fluffy with ripe seed, and with one breath blew the seeds out into the wind. Then she asked Mary to gather the flying bits together again. Mary said, "But I cannot now." The teacher said sorrowfully, "Nor can you capture again all the seed of gossip about Jane that you started flying with one little lie."

> "Boys flying kites haul in their white winged birds,
> But you can't do that when you are flying words.
> Thoughts unexpressed may sometimes fall back dead,
> But e'en God can't kill them when they're said."
>
> **AUTHOR UNKNOWN.**

Even if it be true

The Christian does not say unkind things about anyone, even if they be true. If he cannot speak well of someone, he does not speak at all. Only if he is sure that he is speaking in love, and that by speaking he can help someone, only then will he be moved to speak at all. He is no ready "tell-tale." He tries rather to find some excuse for the other fellow, and puts the best possible interpretation upon what others say and do.

Let's talk about the weather

When people get together, they ought to be able to talk about something other than people. Usually if they begin talking about people they will say something they should not have said. It would then be better to talk even about the weather. Christ was very emphatic about warning "judge not, that ye be not judged." Even the people we know best may have hidden sorrows and temptations which if we knew and understood would change our whole outlook about them. It is best not to say a thing about them, unless we can say things that are good.

The salt of the earth

There are some people we like to be with. They are generous with their praise and gratitude, stinting with their blame. They are quick to excuse men, slow to find fault with them. They see the good in us, and often seem blind to our weaknesses. In fact, they put us to shame often, because they think more highly of us than they have a right to think. In their presence we feel like doing our best. We are impelled to live high and good lives because they seem to expect it of us. They trust us even when we ourselves know that we have not been worthy of their trust.

These are the people the Scriptures describe as "without guile." The world may call them simple-minded and foolish. That matters not. For they are the noble of mind and the pure of heart. They are truly the children of God and the salt of the earth.

What MAY

I *Desire?*

A man should want only that which God wants him to have.
There are two rules we may follow for sure: first, God wants
us to have everything that is good for us, and nothing that is
bad for us; secondly, God wants all men to have the truth and
to be saved. To want or desire that which is not good, or that
which keeps us from salvation, is therefore always wrong.

One thing is sure

GOD wants us to have Him. He may want us to have
other people and other things, too. But of those we can
be only partly sure. Only one thing is always sure: He
wants us to belong to Him, and He to us.

Parents and loved ones

Normally, God wants us to have folks and friends. Sometimes, in His wisdom, He sees it best that we lose our folks
and our friends. If they stand between us and God, He may
take them away. It is possible that a man may be so satisfied

with his dear ones that he sees no need of God. Then one day God lets them be taken from him. With them gone, man may turn to the friendship and protection and love of God. You see, even the normal desire for dear ones may turn out to be sinful desire if it blocks out God from reaching us.

Money and things

Jesus once said, "The love of money is the root of all kinds of evil." That goes for rich and poor alike. For, you see, a man may love the money he has, or he may love the money he does not have. Both are sinful. Money and things are never mine. If I have 50c in my pocket, that 50c really is not mine. If I own a bicycle or a radio or a dress, those things are not really mine. All belong to God. We are but stewards, managers for God. We ought never to love money or things as if they were ours, or might become ours. A clear understanding of this basic truth will help to keep us from coveting.

All money and things are but means to some end; and, because they belong to God, they ought to be means to God's end. Some men love money just so they can pile it up high. And foolishly, many people think that the man who has the biggest pile is the most successful man. Men who hoard money are as silly as the boy who buys a football but never plays with it, or the boy who buys a bicycle but never rides it.

"For I have learned, in whatsoever state

There was once a man who died penniless. There was hardly enough left to bury him. But during his lifetime, he had given over $150,000 to the church. It was said of Abraham Lincoln that he had made over a million dollars, but had never collected it. These men knew that money is God's; and whatever happened to fall into their hands, they used for God. A man's wealth, after all, must be measured not by how much he grasps with his hands but by how much he gives with his hands. It is with man as with a factory or a farm: wealth is measured by the output, by the capacity to produce and distribute.

Defending my rights

A Christian has the same rights under the law of the land as the non-Christian. But the Christian is a strange creature. He often forgets to defend his rights. In fact, he seems more concerned about the rights of his friends, even his enemies. Instead of coveting that which rightly belongs to his neighbor, he reverses the picture. He is anxious to defend the rights of his neighbor; and often goes so far as to concede to his neighbor much more than really is his. A Christian often lends money and never collects it, meets unreasonable demands and never grumbles about it, is cheated out of his rights and never goes to court about it. He has learned that the treasures of

I am, therewith to be content." Phil. 4:11

this earth are not important, and that to be constantly jealous of his rights, both property and personal, makes him unhappy.

To be unhappy

One sure way to be unhappy is always to be desiring what other people have. If you have an old car, you can be miserable by constantly desiring a new one. If you have an old dress, you can torture yourself by looking at other girls' dresses and wanting them. If you have poor skates, you can rob yourself of any pleasure in skating by always wishing for new ones. Many boys and girls have become sour and bitter, and have lost their smiles and their friends by always looking longingly at what other boys and girls have, and wanting something they themselves do not have. To covet is a sure way to be unhappy.

To be satisfied

The Christian tries to be content, whether he has little or much. He has learned that one does not need a big allowance to be happy. If his friends have new things and he has not, he does not pout. If they can take trips, live in costly homes, and get every new gadget whenever they want to, it does not disturb him. He has learned to enjoy the simple things. He is thankful to God for his health, for his parents and friends, for his school and his church, for the sunshine and the rain, the trees and the valleys. Above all, he is thankful that he has God, and that God cares for him as much as for the greatest king that ever lived. The things of this world are second-rate with him. If he is rich, he takes care of his plenty for God; if he is poor, he takes care of his little for God. He remembers that all things belong to God. And when he dies, there are no great attachments on earth that must be cruelly severed before he can go. He goes gladly, for God has in life been his great desire.

56

How Much

Does GOD Ask?

CHAPTER 16 · ". . . WITH ALL THY HEART . . . SOUL . . . MIND"

He says, "My son, give me thine heart." He asks ALL! *He will not take less!*

This means simply that you must love Him with all your heart, with all your soul, with all your strength, and with all your mind. Even should you bestow all your goods to feed the poor and should give your body to be burned, but did not love God like that, you would not have given Him what He asks.

We need daily to ask His forgiveness for not giving Him what He asks; we need daily to ask His help so that we more and more can grow in this love for Him.

Must I give it up?

Y ES, you must! Everything! It may be good. It may be bad. Whatever it is, you must give it up—all of it. You may get it back. Then again, you may not. It all depends on whether you really want it back. Sometimes when you give away something, you discover that you actually do not want it again.

Whatever it may be, Christ asks you to give it up. He want all or nothing. And it is the nature of faith to give Him al In fact, faith means to trust Him for all things, and in turn to give Him all things.

You give Him your life. You would die for Him, if H asked it. Most likely He will not ask it. It is more likely tha He will give the life back to you, so that you may employ for Him. You give Him your hopes. If they be high and nobl enough, He returns them to you for you to realize. You giv Him your abilities. He will not tuck them away in heave somewhere, but will give them back to you, and guide an help you to put them to their greatest use.

Possibilities of Youth

Yes, as a Christian you give Him everything. You give Hir your father and mother; and, while He does not snatch ther up to heaven instantly, in returning them to you, He assign you the task of serving them and making their lives happ You give Him your friends, and in receiving them again yo hear the charge, "Henceforth you are your friends' keeper.

Be not stifled by trifles

Altogether too often the glorious venture of following Chri becomes stifled by trifles. Some well-meaning person says tha to be a Christian a person must give up the movies, card smoking, dancing, and a host of other things. Of course yo have to give them up. A thousand times more than that yo have to give up. You surrender *all!* You turn everything ove to Him who gave His all for you.

Nobody can tell you what you are to get back. Only Chri in His Word, and by His Holy Spirit, can tell you that. If yo read His Word with prayer, and with a willingness to go th whole way, whatever the cost, you will know. Not even you pastor can tell you in each instance what you may do or may not do. You are free, even from him. It is Christ alone who must determine what you are to have back. You are free *in* Him; but you are not free *from* Him.

It would be comfortable if you could settle the whole question by asking someone, "Now that I am a Christian, may I dance, may I attend movies, may I play bridge?" Your church does not believe in settling those questions for you. It is your business to settle them for yourself, before God. The church and Christian people may advise and help you, but they cannot decide for you. On the other hand, the opinion of the church ought to receive from you a most earnest and reverent consideration.

Once Peter let the people think that it made a lot of difference what kind of meat the children of God might eat. This made Paul indignant. He was disappointed because Peter and some other Christians were losing themselves in trifles. Paul thought that in such matters each Christian should have the right, and the duty, to decide for himself, and should in turn respect the right of every other Christian to do likewise. There were other things so overwhelmingly more important. There was a world to be won for Christ. There was the glory of a kingdom to be shared.

One thing you may keep

There is only one thing you need not give up. Christ Himself you may keep. There is no power in this vast universe that can take Him away from you against your will. You may be persuaded with Paul that neither death, nor life, nor angels, nor principalities, nor things present, nor things to come, nor powers, nor height, nor depth, nor any other creature, shall be able to separate you from Him. You will learn with Paul, too, that you can count the loss of all other things as negligible, if only you can have Christ.

What is Sin
Like?

There are people who say there is no such thing as sin. There are others who admit that sin is real all right, especially in their neighbors or enemies. To understand the depth of one's own sinfulness, however, is difficult indeed. Only the Holy Spirit can give a person that insight. Even then it is altogether too natural for a person to think that he himself is not so bad It takes careful and constant instruction by God's Spirit with the Scriptures as the text-book for a person to keep seeing himself as a poor, lost, and condemned sinner.

It is like a disease

SIN is not only something you do. It is something you are You are sick, whether you know it or not. Nor is it jus a skin disease. It is deeper than that. It is in the blood stream of your soul. And it is a contagious disease, spreading from the parent to his child. You had it the moment you wer born. Everyone has it, because our first parents, Adam and Eve, had it. Like smallpox, it breaks out into evil thoughts and deeds. And like smallpox, it cannot be cured by putting salv

"Men loved darkness rather than light." John 3:19

on the outside blemishes. The cure has to reach the inner source of infection. It must reach the will of man itself. For until that is reached, new pocks will appear on the skin the moment you seem to have cured an old one. Many physicians think they can cure it; but there is but one Specialist who can. He is the Great Physician, Jesus, the Christ. He does His surgery on the heart of man, removing the sinful heart, and replacing it with a new, clean one.

It is unbelief

Sin produces a general nausea of the soul, called unbelief. A sinful man cannot trust God; he cannot believe in Him or come to Him. He has no confidence in God, because with his darkened understanding he cannot comprehend that God is love. He either ignores Him, wonders about Him in idle speculation, or runs away from Him. A sinful man does not count on God, as a child counts on his father. He hides from God, as a child hides from a stranger or an enemy. His mind is filled with doubts and fears. Restlessly, he wanders about, finding nothing he can believe for sure, nothing he can trust for sure. So he goes through the world a homeless orphan, without the simple child-like faith in his heavenly Father which alone can give him rest.

It is rebellion

God has a plan for your life. He created you to be His child, to do His will here on earth, and to live with Him in heaven forever. But the devil has a plan for your life, too. He wants you to be his child, to do his will, and to live with him forever. Whenever you go contrary to God's plan, and side in with the devil, then you sin. And your sin is rebellion. You disobey your King, and are guilty of treason. Over and over again the sin of ancient Israel took the form of people rising up against the rulership of the true God to follow their own evil ways.

Man himself wants to be God. He wants to be his own ruler. He becomes proud and, like Eve, thinks that he knows better than God what is good for him. God whispers to him in conscience and thunders through the revealed Word, but man goes on heedlessly to plan his own independent life. Not only kings, but all men, take counsel together against God, and replace His sovereignty with their own. But in his rebellion, man does not overthrow God; he succeeds only in overthrowing himself. Like the man who kicks the stone against which he stubbed his toe, you only hurt yourself by kicking against God. Even if every man on earth should remain a rebel against Him, God would still be the King of kings and the Lord of lords.

It is death

The sinner needs a new birth, because sin is death. Sin brings *temporal* death to all; his body must die, whether in childhood or in old age. Sin brings *spiritual* death; it kills all holiness, and leaves a man dead in trespasses. It brings *eternal* death; for the soul which remains spiritually dead, unsaved by the Lord's grace, enters into eternity to live forever apart from the Lord of life. The Scriptures say that man is sick in sin; but they go further and say that a man is dead in sin. A sick man has some life left in him, no matter how sick he is. But in a dead man, all life is gone. When the Bible says, therefore, that we are dead in sin, it means that there is left not one trace of God's life in us. To tell a sinner that he should try to be like God is then sheer folly. For one could just as well then say to Lazarus in the grave, "Lazarus, try as hard as you can to be alive." But Lazarus was dead. And he became alive again because Jesus brought him back to life. Christ gave him another birth, a new beginning. Because sin is the soul's death, the soul must be given the gift of life in the new birth, if it shall begin to grow in the image of God again.

✠

Many people do not believe that there is such a thing as sin at all. At least, they try not believe it. But in every man, even the savage, there is a feeling of guilt when he does wrong. And even when he does not do anything regarded as wrong, there is in him a restlessness and a fear that he cannot explain. He does not like to face the God who sees in secret and who can read even the hidden thoughts of his heart.

There are others who think sin is only that wrong which you actually do. They say that thoughts are not sinful, if you do not do what you think. But Christ says that a man who hates another is a murderer even if he does not murder, and that a man who lusts is an adulterer even if he does not commit adultery. To God even evil thinking is sin.

But deeper than deeds or thoughts is the evil will, a sinful heart inclined toward that which is evil, and disinclined from that which is good. Even if a man could control his deeds and thoughts, which of course he cannot do, he would still be sinful. So deep are the roots of man's sinfulness. It is therefore that the cure for his sin must be so thoroughgoing.

Is My BODY

Bad?

God created everything GOOD. *The sky was good, the sun was good, and the moon and the stars. All things were good. Even man was good; his body and his soul were both good.*

And God created EVERYTHING. *The clouds above us, the earth beneath us, the trees and hills and water around us, the brain and heart and lungs within us—He created everything.*

Only one thing He did not create. He did not create sin. He gave man a chance to choose, and man himself chose sin. Rather than obey, he chose to disobey. Our first parents sinned, and all their children have sinned after them. And when sin came into the world, a thousand evils followed. For sin damages whatever it lays its hand on.

Is nature bad?

MANY men have thought that the world is all evil. They see earthquakes, floods, famine. They see one animal preying upon another, the lion devours the deer, the fox hunts the rabbit, the hawk swoops down upon the sparrow, bacteria overpower men. All nature, as God intended it, however, is good. Yet Scripture indicates that so far-reaching is the damage of evil that nature itself seems to long to be delivered from something which is disturbing it. And God speaks of a day when evil shall be no more and there shall be a new heaven and a new earth.

Some religions tell their people to destroy this evil world. These religions are like the farmer who cures his cow's sickness by killing the cow. But Christianity says that this is God's world, and that we should stay here and work for Him to cure the world's ills until He comes for us. As Christians, we believe that the best way is not to run away from or destroy the world, but to let God destroy the sin within us. And to the degree that God is allowed to destroy sin, to that degree will we and the world recapture the goodness that originally prevailed.

Is my body bad?

Some religions say that the body is bad and that the soul is good. Christianity says that without God both body and soul are bad. An evil will controls both. The body becomes the vessel for all sorts of wickedness. A car is not bad in itself, but if its driver is an evil person, the car may be used for all sorts of evil. A bootlegger uses his car to transport liquor, a thief uses it to haul away stolen goods. But a good man may use it to take his family to church. If Christ has control of our wills, our souls in Him are good. And our bodies become temples where He dwells. Then these bodies, which otherwise might contain all kinds of lust and violence, become carriages for a thousand good deeds. A Christian does not blame the body when he does evil; he blames the disobedient will in his soul, and prays God, not to deliver him from his body, but to deliver his body and soul from an evil will.

Is my mind bad?

Every man has evil thoughts. Yet, by God's grace, every man may have good thoughts, too. We have bad thoughts not

65

because our minds are bad. God saw that our minds, too, were good. A man has evil thoughts, again, because of his evil will. If he lets Christ dwell in his heart, Christ will help him desire the good, and he will have good thoughts. For Christ is the Creator of all goodness. Luther says that thoughts are like birds—you cannot stop them from flying over you, but you can keep them from building nests in your hair. Christ has the power to keep evil thoughts from dwelling in our minds.

What does man create?

He does not create automobiles or skyscrapers or battleships. He only assembles them. To create means to make something out of nothing. And man always must have the raw materials to start with. Even when he paints a picture or composes a poem, he uses the powers of reason which God has provided for him. It is for that reason that the Christian, no matter how productive his life might be, is able to say in truth, "To God alone belongs the glory." For, without the creative work of God around him and within him, he himself would be nothing and could do nothing.

Is God through?

God has not finished His creative work. He is especially anxious to remake you and me. Of course that does not mean that He wants to remake us so that we have three eyes instead of two or fifteen fingers instead of ten. He wants to create in us a new heart and a new life. In this creative enterprise, too, He does not start with something; He starts with nothing. Whether He creates a new heart in a child through baptism or in an adult through His Word, God finds in either instance nothing in the person to start with. He does not, like a person moulding some clay, find the unformed raw material, and then shape it into a new heart. Sin has destroyed all the stuff of holiness in a person, so that God has to start "from scratch." He does not create a new heart from an old one. He creates a new heart from *nothing*.

Why Does GOD

Love Me?

God's love is deep as the sea, high as the heavens, endless as the stars. The child of God is constantly sustained in the faith that "... If I take the wings of the morning, and dwell in the uttermost parts of the sea; even there shall thy hand lead me, and thy right hand shall hold me." He is in continual wonder as he contemplates the length of, and the reason for, God's great love.

Not because He needs me

GOD already has everything He needs. He is all-sufficient in Himself. Most people need the person they love. A person loves his friend, because he himself needs the love of his friend. Life would be terrible without friends. A lover loves his beloved, and feels that more than anything else in life he needs the returned love of his beloved to make him happy. Even a father's love is governed in part by the fact that he needs the love of his children to give him joy. We can say, therefore, that most human beings love because they need the object of their love.

It is not so with God. He could get along without us. But we could not get along without Him—so He loves us.

Not because He finds me attractive

Deep down in his heart no man is attractive. And, since God sees the hearts of men, He sees that man is sinful and full of evil thoughts.

Most people love the lovely and are attracted to the attractive. If a person is handsome, cheerful, and kind, people are naturally attracted to him. They like him and like to be with him. But if he is sullen and gloomy, people naturally avoid him.

That is not the way of God's love. He loves the unlovely and is attracted to the unattractive. Some people say that God sees the good in us, and that therefore He loves us. This is not true. For, while we were yet dead in sin, spiritually and morally ugly, God loved us and came to us. He sees the ugly in us, and yet loves us.

Not because of my possibilities

A teacher once had in her class a seven-year-old boy named Johnny. He was the most mischievous boy in school, and he never studied his lessons. But the teacher thought Johnny had great possibilities. So she was good to him, went out of her way to help him, and was very patient with him. She hoped he would turn out well. After two whole years, Johnny was no better. In fact, he had grown more stubborn and lazy than before. Finally, the teacher lost patience, and gave him up as a bad job.

God is a great and good Teacher. But He does not lose patience. He is long-suffering, and His mercy endures forever. Of course, man has possibilities; he was created in the image of God. But if God should love man because of his possibilities, He must have stopped loving long ago. You see, man has not turned out well. After nineteen hundred years of the Gospel, he still goes to war, steals from his neighbors, and lies about his fellows. Sometimes it seems that he has grown worse instead of better. But God loves him still, simply because He did not love him in the first place because of his great possibilities.

He loves me because He must love me

It is God's nature to love. He cannot help loving. Even if all men turned from Him, He would love them still. He loved Israel when they worshipped other gods. He loved David when he sinned against Uriah; He loved Jonah when he ran away to Tarshish; He loved Adam and Eve when they ate of the forbidden fruit. He loved Judas who betrayed Him, and Peter who denied Him, and the cruel men who crucified Him. He never stopped loving any of them, He never stops loving you. He *must* love.

He loves all men all of the time

There is no love as supremely impartial as God's. Like the sun and the rain, His love falls on the good and the evil, the just and the unjust, alike. Man may close the shutters of his soul and keep the sunlight of God's love from coming in, but that does not stop the light of His love from lavishing itself upon him. God's love is like the waters of a mighty river, flowing ceaselessly century after century, whether men sail upon it or not, whether men drink it or not, whether men think to harness its power or not. God has no favorites. When He singled out Israel as the "chosen people," He did not love them any more than He loved the Gentiles. He merely set them aside for a special role in the plan He had whereby all men should know His love. Nor does He love the man in the church pew any more than He loves the man in the prison cell. He died for all. For each man He paid the same great price, His own life on the cross.

We ought daily to be renewed in the image of God. That means we ought continually to be growing more like God. And if we are like God, we must love like God.

On GOD'S
Pay-Roll

_____

The Christian works for God. He may deliver papers, run errands for the neighbor, care for someone's children after school, or have many other sorts of jobs. But his main job is working for God. That is why God created him and put him on earth; that is why Christ redeemed him and re-employed him.

Some people think that only ministers, missionaries, deaconesses and other full-time church workers are employed for God. Every Christian is employed in God's kingdom. And every job with God is a full-time job. There are no part-time posts in His business. No Christian works for himself six days a week and spends a couple hours working for God on Sunday morning.

When were you employed?

WHENEVER you became a child of God you were entered on God's pay-roll. For most of you this happened at baptism. From that time on, as you grew,

70

"That ye present your bodies a living sacrifice." Rom. 12:1

you should have been playing games as God wished you to play, you should have been obeying your parents as God desired you to obey, you should have been kind to your brothers and sisters and friends as God told you to be kind. You see, even before you could walk or talk, you were an employee of God.

Does God train His workers?

The Holy Spirit is God's trainer on earth. Through the Word and the Sacraments He instructs and demonstrates how the workers should think and work. But He trains you while you work. It is not always so with other work. Before a doctor can go to work as a doctor, he must have at least nineteen years of school. Before a pastor can be ordained into the ministry of our church, he, too, will normally have had nineteen years at school. But when you go to work for God, you start your job and your school the same day. You do not wait until after graduation before you begin working. In fact, you are not graduated at all until the day of death, when you are promoted into the heavenly life with God.

Where are you employed?

When Christ was on earth, He often likened the kingdom of God to a vineyard, a garden where fruit was grown. He never seemed to think it particularly important in what corner of the vineyard you happened to work. The important thing,

71

after all, was that you were working somewhere in the kingdom.

Boys are sometimes very troubled about what sort of work to take up: teaching, engineering, medicine, law, farming, business. Girls, too, wonder whether they should learn music, nursing, stenography. It is well for a young person to discover what he can do best with the talents God has given him. But God is not very concerned about what occupational corner of the vineyard you happen to choose. After all, a person can serve God in any honorable calling. God is most concerned that you serve Him whether as a business man, or as a farmer, or as a doctor, or as a teacher, or as a nurse.

Nor is it important whether you are in a big town or a small town, whether you become famous or whether you are unnoticed. Many a person who has lived his whole life in a small town and has never become famous or rich perhaps has done more work for God than senators or millionaires.

Can sick people work?

Some people are bed-ridden for years. They cannot earn any money. Often they think that they are only a burden. But they may be doing more work for God than those who are well. For by their patience, their gratitude, their kindness and counsel they may every day be bringing the glory of the kingdom nearer those who know them. And by their prayers they may be doing more for God than many hard-working people who forget the power of prayer.

Can you work with money?

Once there was a person who was earning $200 each month. He said to himself, "Surely I do not need more than $100 a month for myself. I will give God's work the other $100." Each year, therefore. he gave at least $1,200 to the work of the church and to the poor and needy. This was almost enough to pay for a young minister's work among poor people who could not themselves afford to have a pastor.

Is church work a special work?

The church is God's special institution on earth. To it He has given His Word and Sacraments. There children are brought to Him in baptism, there the young are instructed in His truth, there lovers pledge their troth in marriage, there young and old come for guidance, comfort, and strength. God does have a special concern for His congregation. Therefore, the work we do in the church has special importance and yields special blessing. Every child of God should gladly and gratefully do whatever task his church asks of him. We can be sure God would have it so.

When is your work over?

God alone knows when you shall stop. Some people are given eighty years or more to work. Others are called home when they are fourteen or fifteen years old, or before. Your work for God on earth is done only when life is done. Since you do not know how long you have left, you must not waste a single day. You ought to live each day as if it were the last you were allowed.

What is your pay?

The Christian does not work for pay. As a child does things for his mother because he loves her, so the child of God does things for his heavenly Father because he loves Him. But there is a reward, rich reward. In the secret of his heart, the Christian knows that the real joy of life comes from working for God. That is reward enough. But he has the additional promise that when the working-day is over, he shall go on to a greater service in heaven. This, the gift of everlasting life with God throughout eternity, is the hope that holds him up, no matter how long the day or how hard the task. And when that day comes, he shall understand better than now that this really was not the pay he had earned at all, but that it was all along the *gift* which God had given him from the start.

The KING

in Disguise

One Christmas Eve, over 1900 years ago, God came to earth to live. For 33 years He made His home with men. Many people saw Him and talked with Him. Only a few really believed that He was God. He was the King of kings, but most people did not think He looked like one. He was so thoroughly disguised as a man that it was difficult to see how He could be God. But some people saw—with the eye of faith—and they knew.

He could have looked like a King

HAD Jesus wanted to, He could have come to earth with great pomp and in splendid parade. He could have had an escort of a million angels; He could have sounded the trumpets of a thousand thunder storms; He could have shaken the earth with a hundred earthquakes. He could have startled all the earth into fear and trembling, and left not one single doubt among the nations that He was any other than God, the King of kings. Instead He came to a stable, born into a humble carpenter's home.

Then men would have feared Him

Had He come in His real power, all men would have feared Him. No king would have dared show Him dishonor. No army would have raised a sword against His host of angels. All mankind would have cowered before Him like frightened puppies. In dread of His might, all men would have obeyed His every wish.

But men would not have learned to love Him

God did not want men to be afraid of Him; He wanted them to love Him. He was more anxious to have one man love Him than to have a million men fear Him. So He came to earth looking like one of them. He knew that many people would misunderstand Him and say that He was not a King. He knew that they would finally crucify Him. He risked all that in the hope that some might learn to love Him. And He knew they could not love Him if they did not know Him. And He knew, further, that they would never really know Him and His love if they were frightened off by the awful majesty of His kingly power. So He who was King of all came looking like a servant of all.

Nor could He have died for them

God could not have died, had He not first become man. And He had come to earth to die for men, so that their sins could be forgiven. He came not only to reveal God; He came also to pay a price for men's sins. To do that He became Himself a son of man. We cannot grasp this great truth with our understanding; we can but hold it as a great mystery with our faith. He became man not only to teach us about Himself; He became man to save us and bring us back to Himself.

"... took upon him the form of a servant." Phil. 2:7

Even after Easter

On Friday He was crucified. Most people, perhaps all, believed that was the end. But on Sunday morning He arose from the dead. Not even His own followers had expected that. He had told them it would happen, but they had not listened. And when it did happen, His own disciples wondered how it could be. He had died on Friday, that they knew. On Sunday He appeared again to them, that they knew. They touched Him, they heard Him speak, they saw Him eat. But their heads were swimming. One day a cloud dipped down and Jesus rose to meet it. Then they saw Him no more. Still they wondered. They gathered together, about 120 of them, in an upper room in Jerusalem. Then came Pentecost. They were sitting together, when suddenly they heard a sound as the rushing of a mighty wind. Tongues of fire rested upon the heads of each of them. They received the Holy Spirit!

Then they *knew!* All the strange things that had happened in the past three years suddenly snapped together, like the separate pieces of a jig-saw puzzle. Now, at last, they were sure that Jesus had been *God!* They realized that He had been able to heal the sick, love the poor, forgive His crucifiers, and rise from the dead because He was God. Now they under-

"Blessed are they that have not seen, and yet have believed." John 20:29

stood that He had died, not because men had crucified Him, but because He Himself had wanted to die for their sins.—All this the Holy Ghost enabled them to understand.

After nineteen hundred years

It was four hundred years ago that Martin Luther wrote, "I believe that I cannot of my own reason or strength believe in Jesus Christ, my Lord, or come to Him, but the Holy Ghost has called me by the Gospel, enlightened me with His gifts . . ." The disciples who lived on earth with Jesus could not know that He was God, had not the Holy Ghost revealed it to them. To Luther it was clear that he could not have known, had not the Holy Ghost told him. And what was true for the disciples 1900 years ago and for Luther 400 years ago, is true for you and me today. If we truly confess Jesus, the carpenter, as King of kings and Lord of lords, it is not because it is reasonable to do so (for it must ever be foolishness to man's natural reason), but simply because the same Holy Ghost has enabled us to believe in Him and come to Him. Through the Sacraments and through the Word the Holy Ghost opens our hearts and minds to confess that "Jesus Christ, true God, begotten of the Father from eternity, and also true Man, born of the Virgin Mary, is my Lord."

77

These BIG,

Old WORDS

There are some big, old words that every child of God should know. Of course, he can be His child without knowing them. But if he is to be ready to give a reason for the hope that is his, he should be able to say something about them. Each word is not so much a neat explanation of the glorious mystery of God's grace, as it is a picture suggesting meanings more splendid than man's imagination can contain.

Atonement

THIS word usually refers to the sacrifice God made in Christ in order to make it possible for man to live with Him again. Break the word down, and you have at-one-ment. After the Fall, man was no longer at one with God. Sin separated them. Nor could God and man be brought together again simply by shaking hands. Man did not want to shake hands with God; he was afraid of Him and was running away from Him. Nor could God dismiss man's sin by simply slapping his shoulder and reaching forth a "glad hand." It

"But he was wounded for our transgressions . . ." Isaiah 53:5

had to cost God something. And in the fullness of time, God came in the form of His Son, to lay down His life to *atone* for men's sins. That is why the cross tells the story of the Atonement, the supreme act of God in paying the price of suffering and death. His life and death constitute the sacrifice once and for all made for the sins of men.

Reconciliation

This word has two meanings. Man and God had become enemies by sin. Therefore, to become friends again, God had to be reconciled to man, and man had to be reconciled to God. Neither meaning in this word must be forgotten. God had to be reconciled, not because He was peeved, but because sin was a violation of His law for the universe. As Creator and Law-Giver of all existence, He simply could not pass lightly over this rebellion against Him. Some penalty, some price, had to be paid by man to remove the enmity. Man had sinned against God; man should reconcile God again. That was only fair.

But man could not pay, even if he would. So—mystery of mysteries—God became man, and as man reconciled Himself to the children of men. Then, as man saw God in human clothing loving him and dying for him—then, man, moved by the Holy Spirit, stopped fighting against God, and became reconciled to Him. So God became reconciled to man, and man to God. Their enmity was ended; they were friends again.

Redemption

In this word we go back to a picture of slavery. To redeem means simply to buy back. Man had sold himself into sin. He had become a slave to Satan, the world, and to his own rebellious will. As a slave, he had nothing to buy with. His freedom was gone, and he himself could not earn it back. Once he had been free in God. Now he was bound in sin. If he ever were to be free again, someone from the outside would have to come and free him. And Someone did come. God Himself came. He came in Jesus Christ. And He paid the only price which could buy man back. Not silver or gold, but His spotless life and His death on a cross—these He laid down as payment for man.

Justification

Here we have a court scene. The court is the Eternal Judgment. The judge of the court is our Heavenly Father. One day, one of His sons is brought in. The charge is that he is a sinner. The law of the court is clear about this charge: The wages of sin is death. The judge is torn between two profound passions. As a father, He wants to pardon His child and set him free. As a judge, it is His solemn duty to administer the law and sentence him to eternal death. What shall He do? His heart is breaking. If He pardons him, He violates and destroys all law. If He puts him to death, His father-heart will break. So—He steps down from the judgment seat, and takes the sentence upon Himself, so that His child can go free. And, as his Father dies, the child is pronounced free! The court has no charge whatever against him; in the eyes of the court he is without sin. His Father was made to be sin for him. And, in the records of the court, he who sinned has no sin charged against him. He is *justified* before the eternal court, all because his Father stepped down to earth, in Christ, and died for him. When we sometimes speak of "the faith that justifies" or "justification by faith," we refer to the fact that God gives us faith so that we can receive the forgiveness and the freedom which God's work in Christ entitles us to have. The word "faith" is used in contrast to the word "works" to remind us that we are free from the judgment of the eternal court because of God's work for us, and not because of any record of good works that we can present to the court. By faith we get credit for His work.

Vicarious victory

This means a victory won for us by someone else. Christ won a victory over Satan. Satan had overcome us. We were beaten. In fact, we were lying on the field of battle dead, dead in trespasses and sin. Then God came, in Christ; and on Good Friday and Easter Sunday over 1900 years ago He won the decisive battle for us. The victory we ourselves never could have won we now receive from God as a gift. With Paul, we can say, "Thanks be to God who giveth us the victory through our Lord, Jesus Christ."

✤

We never can understand fully what wonderful things God has done for us. It is like looking at the stars. On a clear night we can see about 3000 with the naked eye. Astronomers tell us that there are millions of others flung farther beyond in space. However, the stars we do see give us an inkling of the starry splendors beyond, but only an inkling. So it is with these word pictures of God's love. From the little that we do grasp we can live in constant wonder at the fullness which we cannot know until we reach heaven.

81

The Return

of CHRIST

Over 1900 years ago Christ came the first time. There will be a second coming, too. Of that fact the Scriptures leave no doubt. His second coming will be quite different from His first. The first time He came in disguise, and only the people of faith recognized Him; the second time He will come with power and great glory, and all men will know Him. The first time He came quietly to a little village in Palestine; the second time His coming will be heralded from one end of the heavens to the other.

Signs of His coming

NO one can know the definite time that He will come. That Christ made very clear when He said, "But of that day and that hour knoweth no man, no, not the angels which are in heaven, neither the Son, but the Father. Take ye heed, watch and pray: for ye know not when the time is" (Matt. 24:36). He has given us signs or *reminders,* however. These are of such character that they are found in

82

". . . and great signs shall there be from heaven." Luke 21:11

every age. A study of church history will show that in every age, even in the days of the apostles, the children of God thought that He could come any moment. Wars and famines and pestilences are given as signs, and can be found in every age. Other reminders, such as signs in the sun, moon, and stars, and earthquakes and volcanic eruptions, have occurred again and again. Men have found the "antichrist" in every age; they have detected lukewarmness in the Church in every age. Nor can we know whether the promise that "the Gospel shall be preached in all the world for a witness unto all nations" means that every single individual on earth must have heard the Gospel before He comes, or whether the Gospel shall merely be preached generally throughout the world. There are prophecies concerning the state of the Jewish people at the time of His coming, but these prophecies have never been clear in the mind of God's people.

One thing is sure: He is coming

Sometimes the children of God become too excited over *how* and *when* He is coming. It is enough for the Christian to know that His coming is sure. It is not only foolish, but sinful, for the children of God to engage in bitter controversy over the "how and when" of His coming. Suppose two men are

83

waiting at the depot for a friend. One says, "I think he will come on the eight o'clock train." The other says, "No, I believe he will come on the eleven o'clock train." Suppose they begin to argue about what train he will come on, and they argue until they become angry and part from each other in bitterness. The great joy they should have had together in the common hope and knowledge of his coming is now lost in the petty squabbling over how and when he is to come. The Church of Christ should be held together in the glorious hope of His coming, instead of being torn apart by silly debates over the details of His return.

To cease longing is the danger

Those who never even come to the depot to await His coming at all, and those who stand on the platform debating about what train will bring Him,—both are in danger of losing sight of the towering fact that He will come. The churches that no longer talk about His coming, and the churches that waste their time in stupid debate about how He will come, are both on the path to spiritual death. Both have lost the splendid expectancy, the deep longing and yearning, that the true Church should have.

The end of the world

The majority of our Bible scholars have believed that the end of the world will come when Christ comes. There are Christians who believe that there will be a period of time (1000 years), when Christ will rule the earth in a visible manner. The main body of Christian thought, however, believes that this earth will end at the time of Christ's coming. The Augsburg Confession, in Article XVII, says that ". . . in the consummation of the world, Christ shall appear to judge, and shall raise up all the dead, and shall give unto the godly and elect eternal life and everlasting joys; but ungodly men and the devils He shall condemn unto everlasting torments."

The world growing better?

Sin will be in the world until its end. There probably will never come a day on this world when men shall put an end to poverty and crime and war. For that would mean that men would have to end the greed and hatred and suspicion that surge within their own hearts. The Lord told a story about the wheat and the tares, in which He said that the good grain and the weeds would grow up together, until the harvest. He did not say that the wheat would gradually choke out the tares, until the fields were clean. By this story He meant to teach us not to expect a future age of perfect peace and justice on this earth, but that until the end, good and evil, justice and injustice, love and hate, would face each other in constant warfare. There is even reason to believe that as the end draws near the battle between them will be more fierce than ever.

This fact, however, does not mean that the Gospel cannot make the world better. Where men will receive the Christ, the community of men will have more love and justice. When God enters the hearts of men He works a marvelous transformation within them; and, through them, in their community relations too. But until the end, the power of evil will be an ever threatening reality.

Our abiding city

There is great comfort for the weary warrior of the cross in the knowledge that this earth is not the real home of men. One day the battle will be over, not only for him, but for all men. His General, who long ago won the victory on Golgotha's hill, will then reappear to end the war. The guns will forever be silenced, and those who by faith share His victory will be gathered together in the eternal city. The echoes of earthly strife will be silenced, the bodies of all the dead down through the ages will rise, and the children of God will remember no more the anguish of earth in the everlasting joy of heaven.

How the

HOLY SPIRIT

Calls Men

Without God, man is asleep. He sleeps the sleep of death. He walks and talks, studies his lessons, plays his games, earns money and eats meals, but all the while he is spiritually asleep. Even if he lived to be 80 years, he would sleep right on if God Himself did not awaken him. And if he sleeps on, when his heart stops, he sleeps on into eternal death.

How God awakens him

GOD sets an alarm clock for man in His Word and Sacraments. When man comes within reach of the Word and the Sacraments, the bell rings for him. A baby of three weeks is awakened in the Sacrament of Baptism. A man of thirty years who is asleep is awakened by the Word. If a man is never reached by either Word or Sacraments, he continues to sleep unless God has some way of awakening him which He has told us nothing about. But, as far as we know, the Word and Sacraments are the normal bells which God has ordained for awakening man. It is for that reason that we send missionaries to foreign lands; it is for that reason that we bring babies to baptism; it is for that reason we teach the Word in season and out of season.

Sometimes God shakes men

Many men do not hear the bell, even when it rings. They sleep on and on. Then God sometimes shakes them. He shakes them with sickness or disappointment or failure or sorrow. Sometimes He shakes them with good things. He allows something striking to happen to them. Many men can tell you how they had not listened to God before they lay in a hospital bed in danger of death. Others can tell you that it was when they met and knew a good Christian friend that they began to listen. King David did not awaken until the prophet Nathan came with that pitiful story of the rich man with great flocks and the poor man with one lamb, and added, "Thou art the man." Kagawa of Japan said that he awakened when a Christian missionary came in love to him as he lay in a sea-side hovel suffering a dreaded disease. God may use either good things or bad things to awaken men. Sometimes a war, with all its terrible destruction, will lead people to think and listen. Whatever circumstance God may use, in any event the important thing is that man may be stirred sufficiently to hear the bell and awaken to repentance and faith.

When a man hears

Man may turn over and go to sleep again. Many men have done that. Each time they do, their sleep becomes heavier. Like drunken men, soon nothing will awaken them. For there is something called "the day of grace." This simply means that there are times when a person is at the point of waking up; he may even sit up and rub his eyes and yawn. If then he does not lie down to sleep again, he will be saved. As with a man freezing to death, if he then lets sleep overtake him again, he may be lost. You see, the Holy Ghost calls more loudly at some times than at others. Like catching a train when it stops at the station, a person who does not heed the call at the time it comes, may die before the next one arrives.

When a man awakens

If he is awake, he repents. He begins to feel a great sorrow for sin. He hears the Word telling of a law which condemns unforgiven sinners. He hears the Word telling of a God who loves him more than any father or mother ever could. He hears the Word showing him how often he displeases this God by forgetting all about Him, and by disobeying His will. He may tremble in fear to think of the eternal punishment that will come to him, an unsaved sinner. But he trembles from a broken heart, too, to think of the grief and suffering that he has given this loving God. He sees that it was his sins that impelled the Father to send His only begotten Son to suffer; he sees that it was his sins that drove Christ up to Golgotha's cross. And he begins to understand that every day he fills the heart of his loving Father and Savior with new sorrow over the wrongs done and the good left undone. It is only when he is awakened, that he can sing, "Nothing in my hand I bring, simply to Thy cross I cling." He knows that his righteousness is but "filthy rags," and that if he is to stand before the holy God, he must be able to stand in a righteousness not his own. His heart is then ready to hear the glad tidings in the Gospel.

To keep the bells ringing

There could be no more tragic thing than to have the bells stop ringing. Should the day come when the Word of God is no longer preached and the Sacraments are no longer administered,—that day would usher in the terrible silence of death. It is tragic when churches no longer preach the Word, but preach the wisdom of men. It is tragic when the Sacraments are held in neglect or scorn. It is our great privilege and duty as believers to keep alive the Word and Sacraments in our own congregation and community, and by our missionary efforts to start the bell ringing throughout the world.

88

God's
Repair-Work

Sanctification is the repair-work which God does IN the Christian. Sin has damaged him, but not beyond repair. The Holy Ghost is the expert Machinist who can make him run again. Any human machinist would have to give up and throw man back in the junk yard. But not God!

When God redeems man in Christ, He buys him back from the wreckage of sin. But God is not through with him when He has redeemed him. For the moment He has reclaimed him, He begins to overhaul and repair. The good work He has begun in redemption He perfects in a life-long process of sanctification.

From slave to freeman

THE instant man receives God's gift of redemption, man is free. Imagine a slave who is up for auction. A kind man bids on him and buys him, and says to him, "Now you are free." But the slave, though free, may still behave like a slave. You see, he has lived so long as a slave that slavery

"*. . . who redeemeth thy life from destruction.*" Psalm 103:4

has become the habit of his life. He may hang his head like a slave, drag his feet like a slave, tremble before his old master like a slave. But he ought not, for he is free. His old master has no more authority over him. But it is not easy for a slave to spring full-fledged into freedom. So what does this kind man do? He says, "Come with me, and I will teach you how to live like a freeman."

That is precisely what God does in sanctification. He takes the man He has redeemed from Satan, the world, and a sinful will, and He helps him to live in the freedom of God. He helps him to unlearn the old habits of slavery and to learn the new habits of freedom. For when Christ makes a man free, he is free not only in theory, but he is free in deed too.

If God had stopped with His work of redemption, and had not gone on from there into the work of sanctification, the result would have been tragic. For the poor man, though free, would hobble along through life still afraid of his old master, Satan, still listening to him and obeying him, and until the end disbelieving his own freedom. But God has not stopped. He keeps on in your life and in mine until the end, ushering us day by day farther and farther into the wonders of His freedom.

Renewing us in His image

We were created in the image of God. Before the Fall, we were like Him. With the redemption of Christ on the cross, God started making us over again into His image. It is a slow job. It never gets completely done in this life. Until the end, man often behaves like a slave. But, if the Christian will let the Holy Ghost do His work, he can grow to be more and more like God. One sinful habit after another can be broken, evil thoughts can be throttled, wicked desires can be controlled. A certain degree of triumph can enter the Christian life. He who through faith has already received holiness as a gift, can actually become more and more holy in his thinking and living.

Free from something

The Christian is free from fear. He need not fear God's judgment. His guilt is gone. God has forgiven him his sins, and has forgotten them. They are blotted out of God's memory, and the past need no longer haunt the present or the future for the Christian.

He is free from the fear of sin's dominion. Sin will still torment him, but it cannot boss him. God has bought him away from sin, and sin has no right to command him any longer. It has no real claim on him. When Napoleon was conquered in Russia, the people of central Europe were suddenly free from his sovereignty. Upon hearing of his defeat, many people still remained haunted by fears of his power. But they should not have been; for he had been vanquished. On the cross Jesus defeated Satan and the kingdom of evil. Ever since, every man who will believe this victory and accept it as for him, may live free from the fear of Satan's power.

He is free from the fear of death. For death to the Christian becomes but the doorway into the heaven of God where all traces of sin's damage are finally gone. The dark doorway of death becomes the arch of triumph through which the Christian passes to receive the victor's crown.

Free for something

The Christian is free from sin and Satan; he is free for righteousness and God. The Kingdom of God is inhabited by freemen. Slaves cannot serve there, because they are still bound in the service of the old master. But the child of God is free to follow Christ, to serve Him, to love Him, to give Him sacrifices of devotion, and free at last to live with Him in heaven forever.

The pity of our Christian living is that we who are free to do so much for Him are so stinting in our services. We try to get by with doing the minimum of good, instead of being restless to do the maximum. If we do one good turn a day, we think we are doing well, when we ought to be searching for a dozen good turns a day. If we give the church a nickel or a dime a week, we feel satisfied, when we ought eagerly to give until it hurts. If we forgive someone once or twice, our patience is gone, when we ought to forgive "until seventy times seven." We are free for full service in the Kingdom, and we give only a small fractional service. That is the pity of it!

The joy of sanctification

The Christian has a right to expect victory in his life. Day by day, he will know the joy of new powers for righteousness. Evil habits will be broken, and new habits strengthened. While he is always aware of how far short he falls from perfect obedience, he can have joy in the progress he is making.

But the Christian has joy, not from his sanctification as much as from his redemption. Even when he is most discouraged over his own failings, he can be supremely encouraged by the unchanging fact that on the cross Jesus did buy him back, and that Satan and all his hosts cannot snatch him out of God's hands again. If the Christian says "no" to Satan, God will say "yes," and will hold him by the hand until the end.

There are

NO *Neutrals*

There are no neutrals in the Kingdom of God. Christ said, "He that is not for Me is against Me." Either we are for Him or we are against Him. There is no middle ground where a person can be neither for nor against.

Many people think it the mark of great wisdom to suspend decision. And it often is. But the dreadful thing about God is that you cannot escape deciding about Him. If you do not decide for Him, you are lined up against Him whether you want to be or not. There is no thin line between God and Satan, good and evil, on which you can balance.

Like the boundaries of countries

THERE are places along the northern border of our land where there is but one step from the United States to Canada. One instant you are in one country, the next instant you are in another. The actual change in your condition seems very slight. You stand on the same kind of soil, you enjoy the same sun, the same temperature, the same winds.

93

"A double-minded man is unstable . . ." James 1:8

You even speak the same language. But, however insignificant it may seem, the change is a tremendous one. As you put your foot across the border, your conduct is subject to Canadian law, you buy at Canadian prices, you are punished by Canadian courts, you stand under the Canadian flag.

Stepping across the border

Many tourists visiting our northern states get out of their cars and take this step across the border. They do so merely so that they can say that they have been in Canada. Of course they know nothing of its woods and lakes, the broad sweep of its wheat fields and cattle ranges, the impenetrable forests of its frigid north. They touched the kingdom, all right, but they never had the patience or time to explore it. Nor had they reached the point where they built their homes and reared their families and invested their money and buried their dead there. They touched the border, but retired quickly to the land from which they had come.

The one step of decision

There is an old Scandinavian song which begins like this: "Kun et skritt, kun et skritt, ifra verden til Gud" (Only one step, only one step, from the world to God). The burden of the song is this, that with one brief decision a man may move out of the kingdom of evil into the kingdom of good, out from Satan's slavery into God's freedom. This step is not death, for death never conveys anyone to God who has not already by the step of decision come to Him. It is the step that the Holy Spirit mysteriously enables the infant to make through Baptism; it is the step that the Holy Spirit just as miraculously enables the wandering man or woman to make through the Word.

Let us not make the mistake of minimizing its importance just because it takes the form of one step. For it places a man under a new flag which means a new dominion and a new loyalty. It places him under a new law, the law of love and not the law of sin and death. In fact, so great is the step that Jesus calls it being born anew. It is one step, all right, but it means a new King, a new kingdom, and a new life.

From there on

There are well-meaning people who make light of this one step because often so little seems to come of it. They say that Baptism never saved anyone. Of course Baptism saves; it saves every child who is baptized. They say that conversion never saved anyone. Of course conversion saves; it saves everyone who is converted. The Bible specifically states that Baptism and conversion are the expressions of this step which ushers one into a new kingdom. But nowhere does the Bible give the assurance that either Baptism or conversion makes it impossible for a person to turn around and walk back across the border into the kingdom of the world. Nor does the Bible ever state that simply by being baptized or converted may a person know the riches of the new kingdom without long and patient exploration. We go on from this step, on in the daily walk of sanctification, to discover the endless wonders of this Kingdom of God.

The newness of life

There is a sense in which this first step is the all-important one, because by it you put your foot in the Kingdom of God.

You come under the new law of love and the new judgment of mercy, and you walk under the protection and guidance of a new King. But the first step becomes a mockery if it ends there, and you walk not on in the newness of life. One needs to push on and on if one is to get some sense of the mercies of God which are new each morning. No one can point to Baptism and say, Lo, there is the Kingdom; nor can he point to conversion and say, Lo, there is the Kingdom. One has to search in his own heart every day to see the Kingdom stretching out in new glories and new wonders each day. Jesus made that very strong when He said, "...for, lo, the Kingdom is within you."

This inner kingdom

Let us be glad that Jesus put the Kingdom within us, because not even the fiercest enemies of the Kingdom know how to storm the entrenchments of a heart in which God dwells. The enemy has taken the sword of higher criticism and has tried to cut holes through the Bible, reduce prayer to autosuggestion, and slash away almost the entire historic structure of Christianity. It has taken the arm of the law and closed church doors, sent ministers to prison, and burned the books of prayer. But this strategy has never been able to force the bulwarks of the heart possessed of God. And it is there that the Kingdom's headquarters are! Through 1900 years Christianity has always disappointed its foes, for at the very moment when it has seemed that Christianity has been snuffed out, it has reappeared with fresh vigor to conquer its world. "...for, lo, the kingdom is within..."

But if this inner Kingdom is impregnable, it also imposes severe tests upon the souls who explore it. It yields its riches only to the brave and patient spirits who do not languish by the way. To them it opens a life of great adventure here and endless blessedness hereafter.

Why MEN *Do Good*

Christ sees not only the hands of men, He sees their hearts, too. He judges them not alone by what they do, but also by what they think. The police of the city are interested only in that a man does the right; Christ is interested in WHY a man does the right.

Because they are afraid

SOME people are good because they are afraid to be bad. They would like to cheat, but the teacher might see them. They would like to drink, but their folks might hear about it. Such people are good because they are cowards. They behave decently, are honest, work hard, because they are afraid of the punishment or shame or scorn that they would get if they did not do so. They may even try to obey God because they fear His anger if they disobey. It is a sign of wisdom, of course, to obey God even from fear, but it is not the highest motive, nor is it the reason for obedience that God likes to see in the hearts of men.

97

From a sense of duty

There is in every person a sense of honor. A man does the right thing simply because he thinks it is right. He is not afraid to do the wrong, nor does he expect any reward for doing the right; he does the right merely from a sense of duty. Conscience is his guide; he obeys its voice. Even savages in the jungle and thieves in the underworld have this sense of duty in some form or other, though often twisted and perverted. They show the law written in their hearts, says Paul.

Out of sympathy

People are naturally kind to someone in distress. Even the tiger in the forest will help a fellow tiger who is wounded. In every community people will give money to help those in need. Neighbors will help neighbors, friends will help friends, and men will even help strangers who are sick or in want.

In thanksgiving

Most people are glad to return a favor. If someone does you a good turn, in gratitude you will do something for him. You are good to him because he first was good to you. Many people forget easily, however. Often children whose parents are always thinking of their well-being forget even to thank them for it. And many a boy or girl whose father and mother have died feel great regret that they were not more thankful and did not do more for them while they were alive.

Why the Christian does good

The Christian fears God's wrath against sin; he feels the law's sense of duty. But the Christian has another, a higher, reason for doing good. He does good because someone he loves wants him to do good. This someone is God. And he loves God, because he has learned of the great love which God first had for him. He has learned that when God really should have condemned and punished him for his sin, instead God loved him and forgave him. He has learned that this forgiveness cost God a tremendous price, His own life on the cross. Seeing God's great love, and God's great gift of grace in forgiveness, the Christian in return is so grateful that he wants above all to do that which will please God. The Christian does good not primarily because he is afraid, nor because he ought to, nor because in sympathy he feels like it. He does the right chiefly because the God who loves him and whom he loves wants him to do right; and from a heart full of gratitude to God he strives day by day to do the good.

Doing God's will

When the Christian sees what God has done for him, he naturally asks, "Now, what can I do for Thee?" God says, "I do not need anything. I am not hungry or thirsty, I need neither clothing nor shelter, I am not sick or in prison. But some of My family are in want. They live down there on the earth with you. Some of them are your friends, some of them your enemies. If you want to do something for Me, do something for them. For 'whatsoever ye have done to the least of these, My brethren, ye have done it unto Me.'"

You see, the Christian must love and serve all men, because that is what God wants him to do. It does not matter whether they are neighbors or strangers, friends or foes. It matters not whether they know that he is serving them, or whether they are thankful, or whether they do anything for him in return. The Christian is doing good *to* them, but *for* God. He will then be constant in his goodness, because God is constant. His love for others will have a real impartiality, because it is *for God* that he will love friend and foe alike.

It is for this reason that the Gospel has the power to raise the goodness of man to a new level, beyond rewards, beyond racial hatreds, to a persistent power for justice and charity among men.

What **Is** *the Church?*

Christ spoke of His Church, against which even the gates of hell could not prevail. Now, what church did He mean? Surely not the four walls and roof that shelter us on Sunday morning. Nor did He have reference to a denomination, whether Lutheran or Catholic or Methodist. What, then, did He mean?

Christ does have a church. On earth it is called militant, because it battles against all evil. In heaven it is called triumphant, because its warfare is over and it then shares the final victory with its Lord. Its members have their names recorded in the Lamb's Book of Life. Their sins are forgiven, and they serve Christ in love. And while His Church cannot be listed in the census of man, it does have definite marks.

Christ is its Head

THE Protestants and the Greek Catholic Church recognize this openly; the Roman Church recognizes this, too, even though it contends that the pope was appointed by Christ to be the visible head and absolute ruler of His

100

Church. All Christians know that Christ is the Head of the Church, however prone they are to act as though either an Italian bishop or an English king or a Puritan parliament or an individual conscience were head of the Church.

Since it has One Head, Christ Jesus, the Church itself is one in spite of its apparent divisions. It is one, just as humanity is one in spite of its national and racial divisions. All true Christians confess one Lord, one faith, one Baptism, one God and Father of all, who is above all and through all and in all. In Christ all believers are one, no matter how many the external differences may seem to be. For the Church is not the creation of man, but the creation of God through His sovereign grace.

The Word and Sacraments are its outward signs

This wonderful and sacred Church has visible signs. They are the Word and Sacraments. In other words, this Church can be known by the fact that within it the Word is preached in its purity and the Sacraments are rightly administered. The invisible spiritual gifts which pulsate within the Church are conveyed through the visible "means of grace." Where the means of grace are neglected or despised, it is comparatively certain that the invisible Church is not present. For all Christians, therefore, the Church is at once a fellowship and an institution. Each can be understood only in terms of the other. The Church of the Word and the Sacraments is the "earthen vessel" which holds the true treasure, the unsearchable riches of Christ. So closely did Luther knit these together that he said, "If thou wilt be saved thou must begin with the faith of the Sacraments."

It lives in a "Newness of Life"

The Church of Christ thrusts its members out into a new kind of life here on earth. It does not pack up its Word and Sacraments and creep into a cave to await the Lord's coming. It has a decisive ethical power. Its members are not of the

"Thanks be to God who giveth us the victory . . ." I Cor. 15:57
". . . Compassed about with so great a cloud of witnesses . . ." Heb. 12:1

world but they are in the world. This Church is pitted against
all sorts of evil, individual and social; and its members are
pledged to live by the Spirit. In other words, they are redeemed from the clutches of this present evil world in order
that they might walk through all the numerous relations of
this earth in a newness of life. God's holy will has to be done,
even here in sinful Babylon. It is therefore that Christ's
Church becomes the only real revolutionary power for good
that the world knows. The true Church involves the believer
first in a new inner life, a transformation within his own soul;
it involves him also in the stormy social tensions, where the

new life of the Spirit is at war with the entrenched evil of this world. No member of this Church can run away from his strategic role among the whole of mankind.

It lives in an accomplished victory

Within this Church, even in the fiercest moment of the battle, the members sing the victor's hymn. They already have the victory through faith in the Lord of the Church, who gives to them the victory that is His. Even when they are led into the arena to be torn to bits by lions, they are victors. When their faith is scorned, when their love is trampled into the dust, when their patience is derided as cowardice, they are still victors. When they are weak and fail, in the power that is His they have the victor's strength. Even when all they can show is a broken heart and a contrite spirit, in His forgiveness they are yet the victors. No power in hell or on earth can rob the believer of the real victory, for it is his as a gift of grace from God.

> "And should they, in the strife,
> Take kindred, goods, and life,
> We freely let them go,
> They profit not the foe;
> With us remains the kingdom."

The communion of saints

This victorious host marches down through the ages in epic splendor. We who live in the twentieth century are in the rhythm of ages that have gone and ages yet to come. In our company are the dead who have died in the Lord and are now the "cloud of witnesses." They, the triumphant, are one with us, the militant; and we both, in Him, are victors. And in our company this day are the believers in all nations, within all denominations, of all classes. We are the Lord's body, on earth and in heaven. In gratitude we confess "the holy Christian Church, the communion of saints."

The PASTOR

---

*At the head of the congregation is the minister. He is the
shepherd, and the people are the flock. He has a double call.
He is first called of God. At some time in his life, he has become persuaded that the Lord wanted him to do the full-time
work of a minister in the church. Secondly, he is called by
some congregation. He is, therefore, a servant of God and a
servant of the congregation.*

Every Christian a priest

IN the Old Testament days there was a special class who
were called priests. They stood between the people and
God. In the New Testament days, since Christ, each man
stands alone before God. He has no go-between. Christ alone
is his high-priest. Every Christian himself belongs to the priesthood of believers. No priest or minister can guarantee that a
man can come to heaven; no priest or minister can block his
passage to heaven. The New Testament asserts the priesthood
of all believers. In the Reformation, Martin Luther declared

104

the truth that people were free from popes and priests, and could themselves approach God through Christ.

As a priest

When the pastor stands at the altar on Sunday morning he leads the congregation in worship. When he faces the altar, he represents the people before God, in prayer and praise. When he faces the congregation, he represents God before the people, reading God's Word and declaring His will.

As a prophet

As a teacher and preacher, the minister is a prophet. Like the prophets of old, he declares God's judgment and mercy. To enable him to understand the Scriptures aright, the minister is usually given a thorough education. In addition to high school and four years of college, he has four years more at the seminary. He must know something of the ancient languages, the great teachings of Christendom, and have a general knowledge of the thought of all ages. Above all, he must be able to find and explain the meaning of the Scriptures, for it is there that God fully reveals His will. In the Sunday pulpit, before his confirmation class, in his addresses to organizations, and in his conversations with individuals, he is the teacher of God's message. If his own heart and mind are yielded to the work of the Holy Spirit, he becomes a prophet indeed.

The ordination of the pastor

When a man has heeded the call of God, when he has prepared himself for the work, and when he has received a call from some congregation, he is *ordained* into the office of the ministry. The Church of God thereby appoints and consecrates and commissions him to his task. The Church may thereafter revoke his ordination only under the most severe charges. If a minister is shown to teach error, or if he is shown to be living an immoral life, or if it is evident that he is lazy and negligent of his duties, the Church may remove him from the ministry. This does happen, though not frequently, for it must be remembered that the minister is a human being and is tempted to sin as are all others.

The pastor's duty to his congregation

The pastor is to preach the Word and administer the Sacraments. He must teach and admonish the young and old. He must visit the sick and dying; he must encourage and comfort the discouraged; he must declare God's judgment against the sinful and negligent; he must try to bring the unchurched into the fold. He must constantly remember his people in prayer to God. Under Christ, who is the real Head of the Church, the minister is the spiritual head of the congregation.

The congregation's duty to their pastor

The people must pray for their pastor, encourage him, advise him, and be eager to help him. His task is often a lonely one, and nothing can break his spirit and heart as surely as to be surrounded by a congregation of people indifferent to the spiritual work of the church. Nor can anything on earth so sustain him as a congregation of people willing to attend the services regularly, teach in the Sunday school, assume cheerfully the leadership of organizations, visit the sick and unchurched; in short, people who are glad to do any task, big or little, in the church. There is much truth in the statement that a congregation which thinks it has a poor pastor may transform him into a great pastor if they will pray and work for him.

How to address the pastor

Some people call the minister "Reverend"; others "Mr." Probably the best way to address the minister is to say "Pastor." Instead of saying "Reverend Olson" or "Mr. Olson" or "Dr. Olson," say simply "Pastor Olson." If he thinks as highly of his office as he ought to think, even if he has a doctor's degree, he very likely will rather have you say "Pastor" than "Doctor."

When DEATH
Comes

We really are not on LIFE's *journey; we are on* DEATH's *journey. The moment a baby is born, it begins its trip to death. Every tick of the clock and every beat of the heart is like the clicking of the rails as the train of time speeds on to death. Longfellow stated it with pointed beauty,*

> *"Art is long, and time is fleeting,*
> *And our hearts, though stout and brave,*
> *Still, like muffled drums are beating*
> *Funeral marches to the grave."*

Whether a man is poor or rich, stupid or wise, weak or strong, he has the same ticket as every other traveler. On this train of time, all tickets read "to death." That is where the train stops, and all passengers get off.

Down through the centuries, all men have had a suspicion that the depot marked "Death" is really not the end of the line at all. Rather, it may be just a place where people change trains.

"Remember now thy creator in the days of thy youth ...

The Bible makes no guess about it. It clearly states that death is not the last terminal. Instead of stopping there, every passenger is ushered on to one of two trains waiting to take him farther—on the eternal lap of the journey. One train goes down to the kingdom of Satan, the other surges up to the Kingdom of God.

Who goes where?

NO one buys a new ticket at the station of death. By the time a man steps off the train of time, his ticket already shows what train he takes from that point on. For, during the voyage, the Conductor has repeatedly been through the coaches to mark the tickets of those who wished to go on into the Kingdom of God. Again and again, He has gone through, asking if there were any who wished to go on into heaven. There are those who have heeded His call. Their tickets He has marked with a cross. They then are the "saved." The Conductor pauses to tell them about the glories of the heavenly kingdom, and they become eager to get on the other train.

But many do not hear the Conductor. They are too en-

108

because man goeth to his long home." Ecc. 12:1, 5

grossed in the scenery, too busy talking, too interested in the "game of life" to listen. Some, overhearing the Conductor's call, think to themselves, "Of course I want to go to heaven. But I am too busy to have the Conductor mark my ticket now. I will wait till He comes around again." They put it off. And probably, before they know it, the train stops, and they must get off. Then it is too late. And all those with unmarked tickets are ushered on the train going down.

On to God

The wonderful thing about the train going up is that it leads to the place where God lives. There are many magnificent things about heaven, but the greatest is simply that God is there. Your home on earth is like that, because no matter how fine it might be, if mother or father were not there, it would not be home. It is the same with the heavenly home. If we could not find our Father there when we came, we would not care much to be there, no matter how beautiful it might be.

On without God

The train that goes down takes its passengers forever away from God. And the terrible thing about hell is that God never comes there. People who have not in faith had their tickets marked must live forever without Him. On the train of time many people think they can get along very nicely without God, just as a little boy in his play thinks he does not need his mother. But when night comes, it is different. Then the little boy cries for his mother, and is miserable until she comes. When the night of death comes, people who have gone through life's day thinking they did not need their heavenly Father will know better. But then it will be too late. And their misery will never end, for the train will have taken them to a place where God cannot come.

The grave

When death comes, the body is laid to rest in the grave. The soul goes on to the next train alone. But the hour is coming when all that are in the graves shall hear His voice, and shall come forth. On that day the body, too, will take the train to rejoin the soul. The bodies on God's train will no longer be sick or crippled, they will never again be in pain, or die. These bodies will then have the perfection and glory God gave them before sin came to damage them.

The fear of death

The Christian does not want to die, but neither does he fear death. He is happy for the years God gives him on the earth; but he is happy also in the prospect of the life everlasting that awaits him after death. For the Christian, death is not the end of life; it is the real beginning of life. He passes from death to life. For Christ has assured him that "he that liveth and believeth on Me shall never die."

Because YE *Ask Not*

CHAPTER 31 · "LORD, TEACH US TO PRAY"

Jesus once said, "Ye have not, because ye ask not." That seems simple enough. It is as if one should say, "You have no coal, because you forgot to order coal." Of course, prayer is not really as simple as that. It is more than lifting the receiver and putting in a call to heaven for everything we want. Prayer is talking with God. And while it is so simple that even a child may pray, it is at the same time so full of wonder that the wisest man cannot exhaust its possibilities.

"Cast your cares upon the Lord"

PRAYER is unloading something. Many of the burdens which people bear are needless loads. The Lord wants to carry them. A little girl once had her own version of the 23rd Psalm: "The Lord is my Shepherd; I should worry." Nor was it such a wrong version. The Lord wants to relieve us of the anxieties and worries that weigh us down.

111

The camel at the close of day
Kneels down upon the sandy plain
To have his burden lifted off,
And rest again.

My soul, thou too shouldst to thy knees
When daylight draweth to a close,
And let thy Master lift thy load,
And grant repose.
Else how canst thou tomorrow meet,
With all tomorrow's work to do,
If thou thy burden all the night
Dost carry through?

"What wilt Thou have me to do?"

This verse has a contrasting thought in closing:

The camel kneels at break of day,
To have his guide replace his load,
Then rises up anew to take
The desert road.
So thou shouldst kneel at morning's dawn
That God may give thee daily care,
Assured that He no load too great
Will make thee bear.

—TEMPLE.

Prayer, you see, is not alone an unloading; it is also a loading. It is standing ready to listen to the will of God, eager to assume any task He gives, unafraid of any duty He may impose.

"Go into thy closet"

In prayer we stand alone before God. Whether we are hidden behind closed doors or whether we stand among hundreds of people at morning worship, we should be aware alone of God's presence. Jesus was afraid of people praying in public, for often they would be more aware of the people who heard them than of the God to Whom they were speaking. The Christian is not necessarily the person who has no fear of praying aloud at a meeting; the Christian is the person who,

"... by prayer and supplication, with thanksgiving." Phil. 4:6

whether alone in his room or assembled with fellow Christians, earnestly seeks the presence of God.

"... Prayer ... with thanksgiving"

When a person is still a child, he often forgets to thank his parents for things. The older he grows, normally the more thankful he becomes. When he is young, he is always asking for things; when he becomes older, he is always thanking for things. It is so in a person's Christian life, too. The more mature he becomes spiritually, the more his prayers become prayers of thanksgiving. He catches the meaning of the apostle Paul, "In nothing be anxious; but in everything by prayer and supplication, with thanksgiving, let your requests be made known unto God." He understands that God has given him so many things long before he himself has asked for them,

113

that there is nothing left to do but to give unceasing thank
to the Lord.

"Ask and ye shall receive"

Will I always receive an answer to my prayer? Yes, always
Sometimes it may be long in coming; but always you will be
answered. The answer may be "no." For God knows better
than you what would be best for you.

" . . . As children ask of their father"

There is a great difference between the prayers of the be
lievers and the non-believers. A child of God prays in faith
and trust; he prays to his Father. A child of the world pray
in fear and doubt; he prays to a stranger. To the child of God
prayer is the natural, spontaneous cry of the soul; to the child
of the world prayer is artificial and stiff, unnatural and hard
Just to the degree that faith and trust are present is a prayer
pleasing to God. A person who prays only when he is fright
ened, and as a last resort cries out to a God Whom he does no
know as a kind and loving Friend—such a person cannot be
said really to pray. But if the cry is in faith, even though the
faith be weak and faltering, that cry is in truth a prayer.

"Pray without ceasing"

A person cannot kneel in prayer from morning to night. He
must work and eat and play and sleep. But there is a sense in
which a person need never stop praying. If when he receive
something good his first reaction is to thank God for it; i
when he confronts something difficult his first impulse is to
seek God's help in it; if when he has done wrong his firs
thought is to seek God's forgiveness for it; in short, if God i
so near that he ushers all life up to His Throne in prayer
then he can be said to pray without ceasing.

The Danger
of PRAYING

---

*Few people are afraid to pray. Most people think "There's no
harm in asking." But all people would pray with fear and
trembling, if they dared pray at all, should they think soberly
about what they ask.*

*Take the "Lord's Prayer" as an instance. Are you sure that
you want God's will to be done, and not your will? Have you
thought seriously about having the Kingdom come—how
many habits and plans you would have to let go?*

*Suppose God should take you at your word one morning as
you mumbled through His prayer. After all, He could. He is
almighty, and in an instant could do what you ask of Him.*

*Of course, there's a rub somewhere. Christ has said that what
we ask Him, BELIEVING, that He will do. We are safe as long
as we do not pray believing prayers. The reason why so little
actually happens when we pray is that the willingness and
power of God to answer prayer are held off at arm's length by
unbelief. We do not let Him get near us to do the things we
ask Him to do.*

115

Men who have invited trouble

THERE have been men who have prayed, believing. They have said, "Thy will be done," and have stood ready to see it done. Paul said it, and became a vagabond of God up and down the countries of the Mediterranean, and finally died a martyr's death. Luther said it, and God thrust him out to face the hatred and the scorn of his own church. Livingstone said it, and made his bed and his grave among the savages of Africa. And before any of these men, Christ Himself said it one evening in Gethsemane's garden, and the next day trudged His lonely way up to a cross.

In the presence of God

Prayer is communion with God, and communion with God means facing God. It is never comfortable to face someone you have wronged. And every man has wronged God. Standing face to face with God in prayer means breaking down before Him, confessing the wrong in shame and sorrow, and asking for forgiveness. Nor is that easy. About the hardest thing for a person to do is to ask forgiveness. If you do not believe it, try it sometime. Ask pardon from your father or mother, or from your teacher, or from your friend. If you have really wronged someone, you will know that you can hardly begin asking favors of that person again until the wrong has been cleared up. Nor is there any other way to clear it up than by repentant confession and by forgiveness. When a man prays, therefore, he runs head on into the danger of repentance.

The dread of righteousness

If a man wants to keep on doing wrong, the last person he wants to be with is a friend who wants him to stop doing wrong. Especially is this true if the good man happens to know all about the sins of his friend. And the more genuinely a friend the good man happens to be, the harder it is to face him. God's friendship for the sinner is infinite. His heart is breaking because of the sins of His people. The sinner's natural inclination is to avoid God, to hide from Him. To come out in the open before Him in prayer is terrible. There is real danger, danger for continued wrong-doing, in prayer.

The "give-me" prayer

When the prodigal son said to his father, "Give me the portion of goods that falleth to me," he was treading on dangerous ground. The father granted him his request, and the son spent his money in riotous living. The mistake he made was not that he asked his father, but that he was heedless of what the father's will might be. For any person to ask things of God, obstinately insisting that God grant him his own selfish wish, is very unwise. To add, "Thy will be done," is to risk the glorious; to pray without adding it is to risk the tragic.

The "make-me" prayer

When the son returned to his father, he prayed "...make me as one of thy servants." A person has grown to rich spiritual maturity when he ceases to ask God to "give me something," and starts praying "make me something." At the same time, he has embarked on the real adventure of prayer.

When a man is no longer smugly self-satisfied, when he is painfully aware of his own shortcomings, and when he is ready to have God overhaul him, then he has opened the door for real revolution. Then everything may be turned up-side-down for him. What God may do in him and for him may be more drastic than he had ever imagined. Yet if in faith he persists in praying "make me," there is no limit to the wonders that God can accomplish. It is dangerous indeed to invite such disturbance, but it is glorious, too. For in such prayer, man gives to God the authority to renew him after the image of God, and to launch his life out into the perilous paths of the will of God.

"Born-Anew

CHRISTIANS"

CHAPTER 33 · "EXCEPT ONE BE BORN ANEW . . . OF
WATER AND THE SPIRIT . . ."

This is really a poor title. Why? Simply because if a man is born anew, he must of course be a Christian; and if a man is a Christian, he must necessarily have been born anew. Christ made that clear when He told Nicodemus that "...except a man be born anew, he cannot enter the Kingdom of God."

Every Christian has two birthdays. One is the day he entered this world and first started to live with men. The other is the day of his Baptism, when he entered the kingdom of heaven and first began living with God. Of the two, the latter is by far the more important. The life which began on the first birthday ends with death. The life which began on his second birthday never ends. It lives on with God into all eternity.

The greatest day in your life

THERE are many great days in a normal life. A birthday is great, because that marks your beginnings on this earth. Confirmation is a wonderful day, because on that day you declare before God and the congregation that you resolve by His help to live with and for Him. A wedding day is important, because it marks the beginning of the home you and someone you love will make. Ordination day, if you are called to be a pastor in the church, is a momentous day, for you are then consecrated to the highest service the church can give you. But none of these days is the greatest. The day you became a child of God is the highest of all. For most of you, that day is the day your parents brought you to the baptismal font and gave you to God, and God through His Sacrament received you. That is the greatest! For on that day you were born anew.

Children of death

A baby is a child of sin and death. Although the baby has thought no sin and done no sin, it is nevertheless sinful. From its first parents, down through the generations, it has inherited death. We are by birth dead in trespasses and sin. If we are to become alive, life must be given us. Something that is dead cannot do anything to become alive. If someone does not come along and give it life, it remains forever dead. That is what the Scriptures want us to know when it speaks of a "birth." To be born anew simply means to receive the gift of life. This God gives the little baby in Baptism.

A baby does not know

Suppose you ask a three weeks old baby after he has been baptized, "Do you feel like a Christian now?" the baby, of course, cannot answer. He does not know, nor does he feel that he is a child of God. But that does not matter. If you ask him, "Do you feel that you are alive?" he cannot answer. He does not know even that. Or if a baby inherits a thousand dollars from his uncle, he does not know that either. Yet he is nevertheless a thousand dollars wealthier. Similarly in Baptism. He has become the heir to heaven, a child of God, simply because God promises that through "water and the Word" he is born anew. Just as God uses parents to bring a child into this world,

119

"Suffer the little children to come unto me." Mark 10:14

so He uses Baptism to bring him into heaven. A child does not yet know his parents, still he has become physically alive; nor does he yet know anything about Baptism, still he has become spiritually alive.

Baptism a teacher

It is God alone who gives life. We do not help God do it. This becomes very clear in infant Baptism. For a baby is helpless, so helpless that it cannot even say "yes." It cannot even say "no." It is wholly at the mercy of God. What is true about a baby of three weeks is also true of a man of thirty years. No matter how old a person is, if he becomes a Christian at all, he becomes one by God's work alone. He himself is unable to do a thing to help.

Further, the significant thing about a baby is that it does not *resist* God. He does not rebel, or run away from Him.

That, too, is a condition which must prevail in a man of thirty. He must stop resisting God, stop rebelling against Him, stop running away from Him. Then God can come to Him. In no ceremony in the church is this great truth about God's way with man so beautifully taught as when a child is presented for Baptism. We are born anew, not through the efforts of men, but through the free grace of God.

Dying again

If the body of a baby is not fed, it dies. If the soul of the baby is not fed, it too dies. Or if, as a child grows older, it refuses the food put before it, it will become sick and at last starve to death. Also, if a man refuses to receive God's Word, the Bread of Life, into his heart, his soul becomes sick and dies. Then, if it shall live again with God, He must raise it from the dead. This He does through the Word in what is often called conversion.

Baptized over again

Once baptized, always baptized! That does not mean that we necessarily remain children of God. It means that if we fall away and die spiritually, we need to be made alive again through conversion in the Word, *not* through a second or a third Baptism. Baptism is first and foremost God's promise, His covenant with us. And, because He never breaks His promise, the promise He made in Baptism once is enough. We need no second promise, no second Baptism. We need but to return to the sure promise of the first Baptism. Luther likened Baptism to a ship. If a man falls off the ship, he needs to be rescued back to that ship. He needs no second ship. It is a distrust of the faithfulness of God to feel the need of a second Baptism.

Becoming a

SPONSOR

CHAPTER 34 · "... WHOSO SHALL CAUSE ONE OF THESE
LITTLE ONES ... TO STUMBLE ..."

After a boy or girl has been confirmed, he or she may act as a
sponsor in baptism. There is hardly a more solemn task in the
Christian congregation than being a sponsor. He is of course
a witness. But he is much more than that. He is a spiritual
GUARDIAN, *sharing with the parents and the congregation the*
great work of bringing up the child in the fear of the Lord.
Only devout and earnest Christians should be called to this
role.

A servant of God

THE Bible does not tell us to have sponsors. And a Christian baptism would be valid without them. But it has been the experience of the church down through the years that sponsors serve a vital purpose. So the congregation charges the sponsor with the supreme responsibility of becoming, next to the parents, the servant of God in helping the baptized child to grow up as a child of God.

122

A servant of the congregation

When parents bring their child to the pastor for baptism, they give their child to the Lord. Further, they give their child to the congregation in membership. From that time on, the congregation has a divine responsibility over against the child. If you are a sponsor, the congregation really appoints you as its representative or servant, and gives you a special job to do. As its appointed agent, you are to act for the congregation. If the child later does not attend Sunday school or does not prepare for confirmation, it is your congregational duty to do what you can to bring the child within the instruction of the congregation.

A servant of the parents

If parents ask you to become a sponsor for their child, they are honoring you more than they could in any other way. They give to you a share in their highest and hardest task. For there is no more hazardous responsibility for them than to nurture their children in the fear of the Lord, and by His grace to usher them at last to the everlasting care of God in Glory. In that supreme labor, they have taken you into partnership.

This role of guardian

In the life of the state we have a role called "the guardian." A man appointed to this duty by his government oversees for the state the temporal care of a minor. He is appointed when parents die, or when they show themselves unwilling or unable to care for the child. In the Christian congregation, the sponsor is the spiritual parallel of the guardian. His charge, however, is not confined to the wants of the body, such as food and clothing and shelter; but his charge is in particular for the wants of the soul, for time and for eternity.

Steadfast in prayer

There is no way of knowing the tremendous influence of prayer. If you, as a sponsor, will remember a particular child in prayer, day after day, and year after year, that child will have a powerful, unseen force sustaining him. The Lord has promised that "the prayer of the righteous availeth much." In your prayers for him, you are more than a rooting section in the game of life; your prayers are unseen hands holding him when he might stumble and guiding him when he might lose the way.

Where the home fails

Figures from the juvenile courts show that six out of every ten of its offenders come from broken homes. Court records reveal, too, that few offenders are orphans. The conclusion is cruelly evident: it would often be better for the children that the parents die than that they separate. The conclusion for sponsors, too, is evident: that their task and their responsibility under God in such instances cannot be escaped. Nor need the homes be broken to call forth the sponsor's duties. Where parents are sinful and worldly, and neglect the spiritual nurture of their child, the person next in the line of duty is the sponsor. It should haunt any Christian to know that the child whose charge he was given at baptism never learns to pray and never feeds on the Word of God. When he consented to be a sponsor, he assumed from God the task of spiritual guardianship for the child; and one thing is sure, God will not hold him guiltless if he fails to do everything in his power to supply the spiritual concern which the home fails to give.

Care in choosing sponsors

It is hardly necessary to point out the care parents should exercise in the selection of sponsors. A parent would never think to entrust the guardianship of his child's estate into the hands of a shiftless, penniless spendthrift, no matter how friendly such a person might be. Yet, how often parents ask someone to be a sponsor just because he happens to be a relative or a friend, forgetting that the most important qualification is that he be a wise and consecrated Christian. Parents, pastors, and congregations need to be very careful in delegating this most important task.

The rights of a child

The child for whom you are a sponsor should have the right to believe certain things about you. He should have the right to believe that you are remembering him in prayer. He should have the right to feel that he could turn to you for help when he is in trouble. He should have the right to trust you, to esteem you, to count on you. Down through the years he should hear from you, perhaps receive some token of friendship and love from you, and should know you as his God-appointed friend and counsellor.

You see, it was not merely polite courtesy that made you a sponsor. In the last analysis, it was God Who made you a sponsor. And it is to God that you must bring an accounting on the Day of Judgment for the precious soul entrusted to your charge that day you become a sponsor.

Confessing

Our Sins

The opening part of our Sunday worship and of the Holy Communion includes the confessing of our sins. In connection with the Lord's Supper it is specifically called the Confessional Service. It is not by chance that the Church places confession at the opening of its services. For no person has ever entered the presence of God who has not done so through the doorway of confession.

More than admitting a mistake

SIN is more than a mistake. If a little child uses his fork to eat sauce, he makes a mistake. When he learns that this is incorrect, he admits his mistake. But this is not confessing a sin.

More than acknowledging a shortcoming

If a boy tries to lift a 200 pound bag of cement, he discovers that he cannot do it. He comes to his father and says that he

126

"They were disobedient and rebelled against me." Neh. 9:26

has tried as hard as he can, but still has not the strength to lift it. He falls short of the power needed for the task. But to acknowledge one's helplessness to his heavenly Father is not in the strictest sense confessing a sin either.

To confess disobedience

If a boy's father tells him to mow the lawn, and he plays ball instead, he has disobeyed his father. If he lives the kind of life which his parents disapprove, he rebels against his parents. In such cases, he becomes guilty of disobedience and rebellion. No person is *guilty* of a mistake or a shortcoming. But a person is guilty of sin. To disobey God's will and to rebel against His way—that is sin. And sin always carries with it guilt. Nor can guilt be removed in any other way than by confessing it to God and by being forgiven by God.

The knowledge of guilt

It is the Holy Spirit, working through the Law, who gives the knowledge of sin and the sense of guilt. If it were not for the Law written in man's heart, and given in God's Word, man would be able to deceive himself into thinking he was "a pretty good fellow after all." He could compare himself with his friends, and conclude that he knew many men who were worse than he. But the Law will not let him do that. The Law insists that he measure himself by what the Law says, not by what people might do. And the Law has some dreadful standards. It says, "...be ye perfect, as your heavenly Father is perfect." It says, "Thou shalt love the Lord thy

127

God with all thy heart ... and thy neighbor as thyself." When a man begins measuring himself by that standard, he knows he is guilty. When, further, he realizes that "the wages of sin is death," fear and trembling overcome him. Facing God's judgment upon all sin, he cries with Isaiah, "Woe is me ... I am undone ... for I am a man with unclean lips."

The loneliness of confession

It is right that we confess the sins of our community or nation. But even then it is our own sin that we acknowledge. It is not my business to confess my brother's sins. That is his business. Christ said we should pay no attention to the mote in our brother's eye; it is the beam in our own eye that should be our real anxiety. When in the Confessional Service the pastor reads, "I am a poor, sinful being," and the congregation says "amen," it means that each person, standing alone before God, makes that confession for himself.

Confessing to whom?

We confess first to God, for all sin is primarily disobedience and rebellion against God. A man may feel impelled to confess to some human being, too. If I have stolen $5.00 from John, I may feel that to get peace of conscience I must confess it not only to God, but also to John. Or one may also want to confess privately to his pastor or to some fellow Christian.

Some Christian churches have the "confessional booth," where people come regularly to confess to the priest. This may have many good points. Our church has feared the regimentation which this practice sometimes involves, and the fact that then confession may reduce itself simply to a polite custom, instead of being a deep cry of the heart. But most pastors are anxious to have their people feel free to pour out their hearts in secret to them. And no pastor would dare to violate the confidence of a sinner's confession to him.

Confessing what?

We confess the wrong that we have thought, and the wrong we have done. We confess the good that we might have done, and have failed to do. We confess specific sins, as well as the general lukewarmness of our hearts. The fact that we go along for days forgetting about God, that we are so slow to love and pray and read God's Word—all that we confess. At best, we are aware of only a fraction of our sinfulness, so that we must confess even the sins that have escaped our notice, but are seen of God.

Confessing in earnest

True confession means that we hate sin, that we honestly desire not to fall into sin again, that we long for forgiveness, and that we are anxious to make amends if it be possible. If a person confesses to drunkenness, but secretly plans to drink again, his confession is not a true one. If a person confesses a theft, but has no intention of trying to pay it back, his confession cannot be in earnest.

Nor is confession true if a person does so simply out of the fear of punishment. One who truly confesses does so out of great sorrow of heart because he has grieved and pained the God who loves him, rather than from fear of the God who may punish him.

Against God

All sin is against God. Whether we have wronged our friends, our folks, our superiors, even ourselves, it is really God we have offended. He is the Giver of law and of life. David cried, "Against Thee, Thee alone, have I sinned, and done this evil in Thy sight." Whomever we have sinned against, it is God's forgiveness we must seek above all.

The door of confession

Through the doorway of confession a person passes to the great open spaces of God's unbounded forgiveness. The bur-

"Behold, I loose thee this day from thy chains." Jer. 40:4

den of guilt is gone, the chains of sin are broken, he breathes
the fresh air of God's great love, and moves on with God in
a new-found freedom. His ears are opened for the Gospel's
glad tidings, his soul is hungering and thirsting for the grace
in the Holy Communion. He is ready to know the height and
breadth and depth of the love of God which passeth all human
understanding.

The LORD'S

Supper

On the cross Jesus gave His body and blood in death to purchase and provide us the forgiveness of sins. In the Lord's Supper He gives us His body and blood to convey to us the forgiveness of sins. The same forgiveness which He purchased and won for us over 1900 years ago He gives us through the Word, through Baptism, and through the Holy Communion.

Explaining a Mystery

IF man should write a million books about what God has done and does for him, he still would merely suggest the glorious meanings that are really there. He could not *explain* them. We are promised that we shall know enough to be saved. God and His ways are the source of increasing wonder to the child of God. He can never wrap up the mystery in a neat package of thought, nor can he ever express it in words that tell the whole story. From beginning to end, the message of God remains a mystery. And the Sacrament of the

131

Altar, though many dismiss it because it seems too mysterious, is no more strange than any other part of the Bible's revelation.

"I'll give you a note"

Let me suggest a picture which may be a rough parallel to what God has done in giving us the Lord's Supper. Suppose I loan a man $50.00. He promises to pay it back whenever I ask for it. Since he is an honorable man, I say to him, "Your word is good enough for me." Suppose, however, that he insists on giving me a promissory note. He wants to put his promise in writing, using pen and ink and paper. I reassure him that his word is as good as his note. But he persists, and says, "If some day you should doubt my word, the note would reassure you." So he gives me his promise in two forms: first, his word; secondly, his note, something I can see and hold. Now, of course, the ink and the paper in themselves are valueless; but since it is his word, or promise, in ink and on paper, the note is worth $50.00. Nor did he promise me one $50.00 in his word, and another $50.00 on his note. It was the same $50.00 which he assured me, but in two forms.

"I'll give you my body and blood"

God promises and gives the forgiveness of sins in His Word. And many a Christian may feel like saying, "Thy Word is sufficient for me." But in His infinite wisdom and mercy God has insisted on promising and giving the same forgiveness through visible means, something we can see and feel and taste. He has done so to give us double assurance that the gift is ours. In, with, and under the bread and the wine, He bestows on us His holy body and blood, for "the remission of sins." It is not a special forgiveness, an extra amount, that He gives in the Sacrament. Nor is the Sacrament merely a pledge of the gift He gives through the Word. It is a means, just as the Word is a means; and each conveys to the repentant sinner the same glorious gift, the forgiveness of sins. If we received only bread and wine, it would be nonsense; just as a piece of

132

paper and a drop of ink in themselves would be meaningless. But the Word, or the promise, which is with the bread and wine, makes the difference. The Sacrament becomes a second means, as the Word itself is a means, whereby the Holy Spirit conveys to us the gift of grace.

God is so anxious that we be sure of forgiveness that He has given us this Sacrament.

Not merely a memorial

Memorial services commemorate something that has happened sometime in the past, not something which is happening in the present. When Christ said, "This do in remembrance of Me," He meant, of course, that the Communion services were to recall the sacrifice He made once and for all in His body and blood on the cross over nineteen centuries ago. But the Lord's Supper is more than that.

It is a present communion

When Jesus said, "This *is* My body . . . this *is* My blood," He threw the significance of the service into the living present. He was not only present historically long ago; He is present sacramentally now. It is more than a memorial service; it is a *communion* service. It is a present means for "the remission of sins"; it is a present means for bringing the believing Christian into real mystical fellowship with the Christ who is truly present with His body and blood.

A powerful pledge

Man not only desires the forgiveness of sins. He also desires the assurance that his sins are forgiven. He wants the peace that passeth understanding. I once stood at the bedside of one who had sinned grievously. He had confessed his sins, to God and to me. I had read and re-read the promise of forgiveness and restoration. Peace would not come. Later that evening he asked again for the Lord's Supper. When he had received the bread and the wine, the visible means, peace came! The invis-

ible grace of forgiveness, and its assurance, became his. You
see, the Lord, knowing how much we need forgiveness and its
consequent peace, instituted this supper for us Christians to
eat and to drink.

Eating and drinking in faith

Every phase of the Christian life is sustained by faith, and
faith alone.

It is by faith that we receive the promise as we *hear* God's
Word from the altar and the pulpit on Sunday morning; it
is by faith that we receive the promise as we *see* God's Word
on the printed page; it is by faith that we receive the promise
as we *taste* the bread and wine in the Sacrament. It is by faith
that we cry to God in prayer, and it is by faith that we do
God's will in daily living. The mystery of the Sacrament
should for the Christian be no more a stumbling block than
the all-pervading mystery of the whole of Christian living.

A God so lavish

We ought to thank our God who has been so lavish in
providing us His grace. He created us because He loved us;
He redeemed us because He loved us. He calls us into life with
Him, and sustains us in that life, because He loved us. And to
make sure that the gift of His love need not escape us, He
established His Church, gave the Word and the Sacraments,
and in the Holy Spirit continues ceaselessly to hold the gift
before us.

To doubt or despise any part of God's great work, including
the Lord's Supper, is to treat lightly the lavish generosity of
God's love. To receive it and to thank Him for it all is the glad
privilege of all His believing children.

FAITH ALONE

How much hangs on this little word, FAITH!

It is by faith that we are saved. It is by faith that we grow daily more like Christ. It is by faith that we receive God's gifts in the Word and Sacraments. It is by faith that we dare at last to stand unafraid before Him in Glory.

Because so much depends on FAITH, *it becomes very important for us to know whether we have it or not. Let us try to describe some of its meaning.*

How it comes

IT comes from God. No one can say, "Tomorrow I shall have faith." For, a person cannot have faith simply by determining to have it. In that sense, it is something like a foolish person who says, "Tomorrow I shall fall in love." No one can either "fall in love" or "fall into faith" merely by wanting to. Faith is a gift from God, through Baptism and through the Word.

135

At what age?

Faith can come to a baby in Baptism. Many people do not believe that this is possible. Nor would it be possible if faith were the ability to understand or believe something. But faith is more than that. It is essentially the soul's inclination and capacity to trust God. And that may be there long before the baby can talk or walk,—long before the baby is intelligently conscious of anything. Of course, the faith that one finds in an old Christian of 70 years seems quite different from the faith one finds in a baby. But the quality of trust and dependence, which is the essence of faith, is in both instances the same. In fact, Jesus warned grown people that they would have to recapture the simple trust that is found most naturally in children if they were to belong to His Kingdom. It is altogether possible that a child may more easily have faith than an adult, because a child need not overcome the many doubts and misgivings over against God's promises that face the grown person.

How it feels

A man of faith does not always feel happy or gay, because there are many sorrows and trials in life which make him heavy of heart. A man of faith does not always feel sad either, because there are sources of deep joy hidden in his heart. Nor does he always feel courageous, because there are dangers that make even the strongest Christian tremble. Nor does he even feel kindly always toward other people, because his old nature yields easily to hatred and bitterness.

There is no one state of feeling which possesses the man of faith. He may feel joyous or sad, bold or fearful, kindly or angry—in fact, he may have all the feelings of mankind. But faith, which lies deeper than feelings, does give a strange inner peace that passes understanding. It is the peace that comes from having one's sins forgiven and from counting on the love and help of Christ. That feeling of peace may sometimes be very strong, and at other times hardly felt at all. But one must never make the mistake of saying that when one does not feel it, then faith is gone.

It counts on God for all things

Faith moves in two directions. It expects all things from God; it gives all things to God. Faith makes a person count on God for all things. It counts on God for the forgiveness of sins; it counts on Him for power to break evil habits and to form good ones; it counts on Him for food, clothing, and shelter; it counts on Him for guidance during the day and protection during the night; and it counts on Him at last for a home in heaven forever. It says ". . . Of myself I can do nothing . . . I can do all things through Christ Who strengtheneth me." It relies upon the promises of God, even though yet untested and unseen. When God says, "This is my body . . . this is my blood . . . shed for the remission of sin . . . whosoever believeth and is baptized shall be saved," the man of faith believes what God tells him.

As a child takes his father at his word, so the man of faith takes God at His word. A story told of Napoleon illustrates this privilege of the Christian. The general was reviewing his troops when suddenly his horse became unmanageable, reared, and almost threw his rider. With courage and great presence of mind, a private leaped out of the ranks and brought the steed under control. Napoleon turned to him and said, "Thank you, *Captain*." The private, quick to realize that when the general called him captain, that was enough to commission him a captain, replied, "Of what company, sir?" The general was doubly pleased, both with his courage and with the implicit confidence he showed in the general's word. He said, "Of the general's body-guard, sir." In an instant this private was elevated to a place next to the great general, simply because he counted on the general's word. It is so with our faith in God, too. If we rely implicitly on what the Lord says, that faith is enough to make it so! If we take Him at His word when He says, "Thy sins will I remember no more," then in our faith our sins are blotted out, even from the memory of God.

It gives God all things

It expects all things from God; it gives all things to God. It is the nature of faith to consecrate all life to God. It is in faith that a person turns over to God his money, his talents, his plans, and his dreams. The man of faith dares to be reckless in giving everything back to God. It is as if a man piles upon the counter everything he has—his time and abilities, his ambitions and hopes, his family and friends, his very life—and then pushes it all over and says, "Here it is, God, all of it; it is all yours." Such is the double movement of faith: it counts on God for all things; it gives to God all things.

Self-confidence

The man of faith really has no self-confidence. He may seem to have all sorts of self-confidence. For he dares to tackle the impossible. But his confidence lies deeper than in himself. It rests upon God. And if he is convinced that God asks him to do something, he has the courage to do it. You see, he is sure that God will not ask him to do something unless He at the same time provides the strength and circumstances to do it. The faith he seems to have in himself, however, is really the faith that he has in God.

LIFE'S

Supreme Aim

The supreme aim of life can be stated in many ways. Some say that "to leave the world a bit better for having been here" is the highest goal for any life. Others declare that "to be saved" is the greatest good. The mature Christian will probably insist that the supreme aim of any life ought to be simply TO GLORIFY GOD.

And the deeper the Holy Spirit pushes us into the mysteries of God and life, the more accurate this statement seems to become. We are here on this earth not primarily to have families and keep the race of men going, not primarily to build roads and schools and churches, not primarily to elbow our way into the shelter of everlasting life. We are here to glorify God

Not merely singing His praise

TO glorify God does not involve merely shouting His praises. It means doing His will in the hundreds of relations which life attaches to us. A lover who thinks that he can honor his beloved merely by telling everybody how charming and wonderful she is has indeed a shallow concept of what honor means. Above all, whether he says much about her or not, he will strive every moment of the day and night to live for her. Only by full devotion can he honor her. Nothing short of that will do if the aim of our lives is to glorify God. Every area of life will be dedicated to Him.

To strive for everything good

God is the author of truth and righteousness. To glorify Him means to exalt truth and justice and love. But let us not put the cart before the horse. We are dedicated to truth and justice and love because we are dedicated to the honoring of God. The reverse is not necessarily true. That is, a man may not necessarily be dedicated to the honoring of God because he is dedicated to truth and justice and love. The person of God comes first, and following Him, "as the night the day," will be truth and justice and love. Christianity is first a person's relationship with God Himself, through repentance and faith; thereafter it is his relationship with the cause of God. It is therefore that to glorify the *Kingdom* of God is not the highest aim, but to glorify God Himself.

Full forgetfulness of self

So complete should be the Christian's desire to glorify God that he himself would be willing to be forgotten. The apostle Paul once said that he was so anxious that God be glorified among his fellow men that he would be willing to be "condemned," to be forgotten even in heaven. The Christian cares not for credit or glory for himself. If he gives gifts, it is that God may be honored. If he loves his enemies, he does it, not to be loved in return by his enemies, but that they, seeing his good works, may glorify his Father who is in heaven. He is willing to be completely forgotten, if through him God will be remembered.

Blocking God's glory

Often without intending to do so, a Christian may stand between God and someone else. The Christian should be a window, through which others can see God. If people see the Christian, and not God, then somehow the Christian has blocked the sight of God. The Christian's faults may mar the view. His virtues may mar it, too, if he be not very careful. Precisely here lies the Christian's most difficult task. In some way he must have people see that he is honest, kind, and pure, not because he himself is good, but because his God is merciful and powerful to help him be good. Your friend's mother should not say to her boy, "You could be a fine boy, too, if you would just be like John"; rather she should say, "You could be a fine boy, too, if, like John, you would let Christ help you." You see, she should be able to see in you, not your goodness, but God's goodness in you.

Beyond self

It is said that Socrates of Ancient Greece had been supremely equipped by God to be a teacher. He had a large, disproportioned nose, a squatty face as if someone had pushed it together from the top, and features covered with black warts. There was nothing physically attractive nor magnetic about him. People followed him and listened to him only because of the truth he tried to teach. His followers became disciples, not of Socrates, but of truth.

Surely the Christian should not himself become the object of loyalty and devotion. His life should attract men to the Lord Who is the Way and Truth and Life, and his friends and associates should through his life be led to the Lord Who alone can give life.

"Hans had a great God"

Hans was a section-hand who loved God. When he died, a fellow-worker remarked to his friend as they were leaving the cemetery, "Hans had a great God." Would it not have been a pity if instead he had said, "Hans was a great Christian"? The triumph of Hans's life was that it really had been a window, and that through him his fellow-laborer had caught a glimpse of God. Hans was forgotten, but Hans's God was remembered.

None greater among men

Jesus singled out one man here on earth as truly great. He said, "Verily I say unto you, Among them that are born of women there hath not risen a greater than John the Baptist." John's greatness lay in his thorough self-forgetfulness. When he said, "He must increase, but I must decrease," he really meant it. For John could have had a great following. Instead, when people came to honor him, he pointed them from himself to "the Lamb of God." He was able to divorce his followers from himself and direct them to Christ. The praise and the popularity he might easily have had he gladly surrendered. He had come to the earth to prepare the way for a Greater, the Christ. And before his death he had the supreme satisfaction of seeing himself abandoned and forgotten, and the Christ whom he came to declare, followed and remembered.

✛

It is of some distinction that your name be honored in your community, that it be recorded on the pages of history books, or that it be chiseled in stone on some building. But the true and high end of life is that it be forgotten, that it fade away to be displaced by the Name which is above every name; and that because you have lived some people have caught a glimpse of the God in whom you lived and moved and had your being.

"Let your light so shine before men, that they may see your good works, and glorify your Father which is in heaven" (Matthew 5:16).

142

Back to

GOD

"He came from God; he went back to God." Such is the biography of the Christian.

IN the foothills of Montana's Rockies, a little stream is born. It trickles its fitful path down the hillsides, and flows out into the plains. Growing broader and deeper, it becomes a river, the Missouri.

Montana says, "River, you're mine." But on it flows, declining to be cradled long by its parent state. Coursing on through the sister Dakotas, it hears again the claim, "River, you're ours." Heedless, it pushes on, angling its way between Nebraska and Iowa, but not before each of these neighbors has reached out for possession, "River, you're mine." Like a restless eel, it slips away, down to join the great Father of Waters, the Mississippi. And as it joins its flow with the larger, the Mississippi says, "At last you have come to me; now you're mine."

Still it flows silently on. At last its currents become slower, fuller, until down into the great Gulf of Mexico it comes to

143

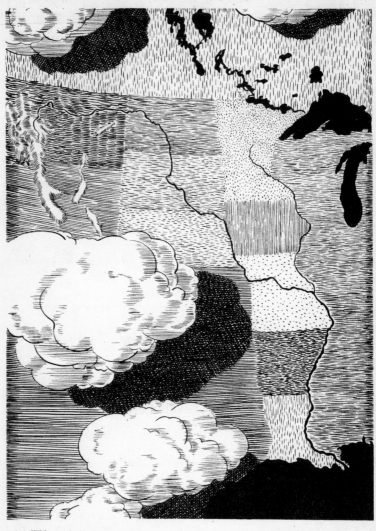

"They shall flow together to the goodness of the Lord." Jer. 31:12

rest in the bosom of the ocean. In the rhythmic heaving of the
deep, it hears the ocean's whisper, "River, you're mine. You've
always been mine. It was I who sent the storm clouds into the
mountains to give you birth. It was I who pulled you steadily,
irresistibly, away from all others back to me. From me you
came, to me you return. Only I can really say 'you're mine.'"

Into a home a little girl is born. Bending tenderly over the cradle, a mother whispers, "Baby, you're mine." The years go on, and soon the baby has become a lady. And a lover takes her by the hand, and a deeper voice echoes the mother's whisper, "Sweetheart, you're mine." Then one day she stands looking into the blue eyes of her own baby, and her mother ears seem to catch the unspoken claim of her child, "Mother, you're mine." But the years refuse to linger, and all too soon her hair becomes silver. Life becomes fuller, deeper, slower, and one day she glides through the narrows into Eternity's ocean. There, in the bosom of her heavenly Father, she hears the voice of God, "My child, you're Mine. You've always been Mine. It was I who gave you birth. It was I who drew you, through My redeeming love in Christ, drew you away from all others back to Me. From Me you came, to Me you return. Only I can really say, 'you're Mine.'"

✝

We have not here an abiding city, you see. Our Father, the King, never intended us to settle down here on this earth. Our real home is in the palace, with Him. The few years we are here are but the flow back to Him. Like the moving waters of a mighty river, we are to give growth and health and beauty to all we touch. But we are not to be caught up into the eddies and flow off into side-pools to rest. We must not become trapped or ensnared on the way. For we do not belong to anyone or anything along the banks. We belong back with God.

To slip away from the steady pull of God's love is the ever-threatening tragedy. If people or money or pleasure should lure us into some side-lagoon, where we would be beyond the reach of Eternity's pull, all would be lost. And that can so easily happen! For if we neglect the Church, the Word and the Sacraments, we can quickly be lured into the comfortable pools of this world. Then the divine movement of life comes to a standstill: we cease to pray, we forget to love and obey, we lose the touch of God. Life is robbed of its freshness, hope and faith are gone, and the days bog down into a weary boredom.

But to move on, what adventure!

We are rivers of living water, fresh with the grace that God Himself pours into us. Each person we touch, parents, brothers, and sisters, husbands and wives, sons and daughters, friends and foes, every person becomes someone into whose life we are to pour the love of heaven. Every good cause becomes an enterprise to be empowered and enriched by the flow of our concern and energy. Every day dawns throbbing with new opportunities for our work in the vineyard. What is around the next bend, we do not know. But we are not afraid of the morrow. For tomorrow, like today, is but another part of the voyage we make with God and to God. And come what may, we have the sure promise of God that nothing shall be able to separate us from the love of God, neither death, nor life, nor angels, nor principalities, nor powers, nor things present, nor things to come, nor height, nor depth, nor any other creature, for we have the love of God through Christ Jesus, our Lord.

✛

One day we shall stand in the palace again. Our Father, the King, will be there. In His hand He holds the crown of life. And blessed beyond words or thought will be our lot if then we can hear from His mouth, "Well done, thou good and faithful servant: thou hast been faithful over a few things, I will make thee ruler over many things: enter thou into the joy of thy Lord."

Luther's Small Catechism

PART I

The Ten Commandments

THE INTRODUCTION

I am the Lord thy God.

THE FIRST COMMANDMENT

Thou shalt have no other gods before Me.

What does this mean?

We should fear, love, and trust in God above all things.

THE SECOND COMMANDMENT

Thou shalt not take the name of the Lord thy God in vain; for the Lord will not hold him guiltless that taketh His name in vain.

What does this mean?

We should fear and love God so that we do not curse, swear, conjure, lie, or deceive, by His name, but call upon Him in every time of need, and worship Him with prayer, praise, and thanksgiving.

THE THIRD COMMANDMENT

Remember the Sabbath day, to keep it holy.

What does this mean?

We should fear and love God so that we do not despise His Word and the preaching of the same, but deem it holy, and gladly hear and learn it.

THE FOURTH COMMANDMENT

Honor thy father and thy mother, that thy days may be long upon the land which the Lord thy God giveth thee

What does this mean?

We should fear and love God so that we do not despise our parents and superiors, nor provoke them to anger, but honor, serve, obey, love, and esteem them.

THE FIFTH COMMANDMENT

Thou shalt not kill.

What does this mean?

We should fear and love God so that we do our neighbor no bodily harm nor cause him any suffering, but help and befriend him in every need.

THE SIXTH COMMANDMENT

Thou shalt not commit adultery.

What does this mean?

We should fear and love God so that we lead a chaste and pure life in word and deed, and that husband and wife love and honor each other.

THE SEVENTH COMMANDMENT

Thou shalt not steal.

What does this mean?

We should fear and love God so that we do not rob our neighbor of his money or property, nor bring them into our possession by unfair dealing or fraud, but help him to improve and protect his property and living.

THE EIGHTH COMMANDMENT

Thou shalt not bear false witness against thy neighbor.

What does this mean?

We should fear and love God so that we do not deceitfully belie, betray, backbite, nor slander our neighbor, but apologize for him, speak well of him, and put the most charitable construction on all that he does.

THE NINTH COMMANDMENT

Thou shalt not covet thy neighbor's house.

What does this mean?

We should fear and love God so that we do not seek by craftiness to gain possession of our neighbor's inheritance or home nor obtain them under pretense of a legal right, but assist and serve him in keeping the same.

THE TENTH COMMANDMENT

Thou shalt not covet thy neighbor's wife, nor his manservant, nor his maidservant, nor his cattle, nor anything that is thy neighbor's.

What does this mean?

We should fear and love God so that we do not estrange or entice away our neighbor's wife, servants, or cattle, but seek to have them remain and discharge their duty to him.

THE CONCLUSION

What does God declare concerning all these commandments?

He says: I the Lord thy God am a jealous God, visiting the iniquity of the fathers upon the children unto the third and fourth generation of them that hate Me; and showing mercy unto thousands of them that love Me and keep My commandments.

What does this mean?

God threatens to punish all who transgress these commandments. We should, therefore, fear His wrath, and in no wise disobey them. But He promises grace and every blessing to all who keep them. We should, therefore, love Him, trust in Him, and gladly keep His commandments.

Part II

The Creed

THE FIRST ARTICLE
OF CREATION

I believe in God the Father almighty, Maker of heaven and earth.

What does this mean?

I believe that God has created me and all that exists; that He has given and still preserves to me my body and soul, my eyes and ears, and all my members, my reason and all the powers of my soul, together with food and raiment, home and family, and all my property; that He daily provides abundantly for all the needs of my life, protects me from all danger, and guards and keeps me from all evil; and that He does this purely out of fatherly and divine goodness and mercy, without any merit or worthiness in me; for all of which I am in duty bound to thank, praise, serve, and obey Him. This is most certainly true.

THE SECOND ARTICLE
OF REDEMPTION

And in Jesus Christ His only Son, our Lord; who was conceived by the Holy Spirit, born of the Virgin Mary; suffered under Pontius Pilate, was crucified, dead, and buried; He descended into hell; the third day He rose again from the dead; He ascended into heaven, and sitteth on the right hand of God the Father almighty; from thence He shall come to judge the quick and the dead.

What does this mean?

I believe that Jesus Christ, true God, begotten of the Father from eternity, and also true Man, born of the Virgin Mary, is my Lord; who has redeemed me, a lost and condemned creature, bought me and freed me from all sins, from death, and from the power of the devil; not with silver and gold, but with His holy and precious blood, and with His innocent sufferings and death;

in order that I might be His own, live under Him in His kingdom, and serve Him in everlasting righteousness, innocence, and blessedness; even as He is risen from the dead, and lives and reigns to all eternity. This is most certainly true.

I believe in the Holy Spirit; the holy Christian Church, the Communion of Saints; the forgiveness of sins; the resurrection of the body and the life everlasting.

What does this mean?

I believe that I cannot by my own reason or strength believe in Jesus Christ my Lord, or come to Him; but the Holy Spirit has called me through the Gospel, enlightened me with His gifts, and sanctified and preserved me in the true faith; in like manner as He calls, gathers, enlightens and sanctifies the whole Christian Church on earth, and preserves it in union with Jesus Christ in the one true faith; in which Christian Church He daily forgives abundantly all my sins, and the sins of all believers, and at the last day will raise up me and all the dead, and will grant everlasting life to me and to all who believe in Christ. This is most certainly true.

PART III

The Lord's Prayer

THE INTRODUCTION

Our Father, who art in heaven.

What does this mean?

God thereby tenderly encourages us to believe that He is truly our Father, and that we are truly His children, so that we may boldly and confidently come to Him in prayer, even as beloved children come to their dear father.

THE FIRST PETITION

Hallowed be Thy name.

What does this mean?

God's name is indeed holy in itself; but we pray in this petition that it may be hallowed also among us.

How is this done?

When the Word of God is taught in its truth and purity and we, as God's children, lead holy lives, in accordance with it. This grant us, dear Father in heaven! But whoever teaches and lives otherwise than God's Word teaches, profanes the name of God among us. From this preserve us, heavenly Father!

THE SECOND PETITION

Thy kingdom come.

What does this mean?

The kingdom of God comes indeed of itself, without our prayer; but we pray in this petition that it may come also to us.

How is this done?

When our heavenly Father gives us His Holy Spirit, so that by His grace we believe His holy Word, and live a godly life here on earth, and in heaven for ever.

Thy will be done on earth, as it is in heaven.

What does this mean?

The good and gracious will of God is done indeed without our prayer; but we pray in this petition that it may be done also among us.

How is this done?

When God destroys and brings to naught every evil counsel and purpose of the devil, the world, and our own flesh, which would hinder us from hallowing His name, and prevent the coming of His kingdom; and when He strengthens us and keeps us steadfast in His Word and in faith, even unto our end. This is His good and gracious will.

THE FOURTH PETITION

Give us this day our daily bread.

What does this mean?

God indeed gives daily bread to all men, even to the wicked, without our prayer; but we pray in this petition that He would lead us to acknowledge our daily bread as His gift, and to receive it with thanksgiving.

What is meant by daily bread?

Everything that is required to satisfy our bodily needs; such as food and raiment, house and home, fields and flocks, money and goods; pious parents, children, and servants; godly and faithful rulers, good government; seasonable weather, peace and health; order and honor; true friends, good neighbors, and the like.

THE FIFTH PETITION

And forgive us our trespasses, as we forgive those who trespass against us.

What does this mean?

We pray in this petition that our heavenly Father would not regard our sins nor because of them deny our prayers; for we neither merit nor are worthy of those things for which we pray;

but that He would grant us all things through grace, even though we sin daily, and deserve nothing but punishment. And certainly we, on our part, will heartily forgive, and gladly do good to those who may sin against us.

THE SIXTH PETITION

And lead us not into temptation.

What does this mean?

God indeed tempts no one to sin; but we pray in this petition that God would so guard and preserve us, that the devil, the world, and our own flesh may not deceive us, nor lead us into error and unbelief, despair, and other great and shameful sins; but that, when so tempted, we may finally prevail and gain the victory.

THE SEVENTH PETITION

But deliver us from evil.

What does this mean?

We pray in this petition, as in a summary, that our heavenly Father would deliver us from all manner of evil, whether it affect body or soul, property or reputation, and at last, when the hour of death shall come, grant us a blessed end, and graciously take us from this world of sorrow to Himself in heaven.

THE CONCLUSION

For Thine is the kingdom, and the power, and the glory, for ever and ever. Amen.

What does the word "Amen" mean?

It means that I should be assured that such petitions are acceptable to our heavenly Father, and are heard by Him; for He Himself has commanded us to pray in this manner, and has promised to hear us. Amen, Amen, that is, Yea, yea, it shall be so.

PART IV

The Sacrament of Baptism

I

WHAT IS BAPTISM?

Baptism is not simply water, but it is the water used according to God's command and connected with God's word.

What is this word of God?

It is the word of our Lord Jesus Christ, as recorded in the last chapter of Matthew: "Go ye therefore, and make disciples of all the nations, baptizing them into the name of the Father and of the Son and of the Holy Spirit."

II

WHAT GIFTS OR BENEFITS DOES BAPTISM BESTOW?

It works forgiveness of sins, delivers from death and the devil, and gives everlasting salvation to all who believe, as the word and promise of God declares.

What is this word and promise of God?

It is the word of our Lord Jesus Christ, as recorded in the last chapter of Mark: "He that believeth and is baptized shall be saved; but he that disbelieveth shall be condemned."

III

HOW CAN WATER DO SUCH GREAT THINGS?

It is not the water, indeed, that does such great things, but the word of God, connected with the water, and our faith which relies on that word of God. For without the word of God, it is simply water and no baptism. But when connected with the word of God, it is a baptism, that is, a gracious water of life and a washing of regeneration in the Holy Spirit, as St. Paul says to Titus, in the third chapter: "According to His mercy He saved us, through the washing of regeneration and renewing of the Holy Spirit, which He poured out upon us richly, through Jesus Christ our Savior; that, being justified by His grace, we might be made heirs according to the hope of eternal life. This is a faithful saying."

IV

WHAT DOES SUCH BAPTIZING WITH WATER SIGNIFY?

It signifies that the old Adam in us, together with all sins and evil lusts, should be drowned by daily sorrow and repentance, and be put to death; and that the new man should daily come forth and rise, to live before God in righteousness and holiness for ever.

Where is it so written?

St. Paul, in the sixth chapter of the Epistle to the Romans, says: "We were buried therefore with Him through baptism into death: that like as Christ was raised from the dead through the glory of the Father, so we also might walk in newness of life."

OF CONFESSION

What is Confession?

Confession consists of two parts: the one is that we confess our sins; the other, that we receive absolution or forgiveness from the pastor as from God Himself, in no wise doubting, but firmly believing, that our sins are thereby forgiven before God in heaven.

What sins should we confess?

Before God we should acknowledge ourselves guilty of all manner of sins, even of those of which we are not aware, as we do in the Lord's Prayer. To the pastor we should confess only those sins which we know and feel in our hearts.

What are such sins?

Here examine yourself in the light of the Ten Commandments, whether as father or mother, son or daughter, master or servant, you have been disobedient, unfaithful, slothful, illtempered, unchaste, or quarrelsome, or whether you have injured any one by word or deed, stolen, neglected, or wasted aught, or done any other evil.

PART V

The Sacrament of the Altar

I

WHAT IS THE SACRAMENT OF THE ALTAR?

It is the true Body and Blood of our Lord Jesus Christ, under the bread and wine, given unto us Christians to eat and to drink, as it was instituted by Christ Himself.

Where is it so written?

The holy Evangelists, Matthew, Mark, and Luke, together with St. Paul, write thus:

"Our Lord Jesus Christ, in the night in which He was betrayed, took bread; and when He had given thanks, He brake it and gave it to His disciples, saying, Take, eat; this is My Body, which is given for you; this do in remembrance of Me.

"After the same manner, also, He took the cup, when He had supped, and when He had given thanks, He gave it to them, saying, Drink ye all of it; this cup is the new testament in My Blood, which is shed for you, and for many, for the remission of sins; this do, as oft as ye drink it, in remembrance of Me."

II

WHAT IS THE BENEFIT OF SUCH EATING AND DRINKING?

It is pointed out in these words: "Given and shed for you for the remission of sins." Through these words the remission of sins, life and salvation are given unto us in the Sacrament; for where there is remission of sins, there is also life and salvation.

III

HOW CAN THE BODILY EATING AND DRINKING PRODUCE SUCH GREAT BENEFITS?

The eating and drinking, indeed, do not produce them, but the words: "Given and shed for you for the remission of sins." For besides the bodily eating and drinking, these words are the chief thing in the Sacrament; and he who believes them has what they say and declare, namely, the remission of sins.

IV

WHO, THEN, RECEIVES THE SACRAMENT WORTHILY?

Fasting and bodily preparation are indeed a good outward discipline, but he is truly worthy and well prepared who believes these words: "Given and shed for you for the remission of sins." But he who does not believe these words or who doubts them is unworthy and unprepared; for the words: "For you," require truly believing hearts.

5240